ABOUT THE AUTHOR

Anthony Rizk has been a student and researcher of human behavior patterns, lateral thinking, behavioral change, NeuroLinguistic Programming and hypnosis for many years. He holds a Masters in Business Administration, and is NGH Certified, a peak performance strategist and coach, a NeuroLinguistic Programming Trainer, a corporate trainer and a motivational speaker.

He operates out of Lebanon where he has successfully conducted thousands of coaching sessions. In addition to his clients, famous celebrities, politicians, high profile professionals, and leading companies consult him regularly seeking to overcome personal challenges and realize their true potential.

Anthony's passion is to figure out what makes people successful, and how to develop ways to mold the success of others into easy to apply strategies. Moreover, he has helped put together a NeuroLinguistic Programming course exclusively for business professionals, and received the complete approval of the National Federation of NeuroLinguistic Programming, hence allowing him to fully train and certify practitioners from all walks of life. In addition, Anthony has engaged in several motivational events where he introduced the concept of edutainment in the region, a mixture between education and entertainment.

As you will experience soon, Anthony's recordings, sessions, trainings, lectures and events are consistently the most effective, popular and trusted of their type.

For more information about the author, visit www.anthonyrizk.org

An easy and practical guide
to transforming your life

THE
POWER
OF LIFE
MASTERY

ANTHONY RIZK

Dedicated to you my dear reader and to your inspired mind which has the infinite ability to co-create your destiny.

Most of all for me, to my beloved family.

ACKNOWLEDGMENTS

I would like to express my gratitude to the many people who saw me through this book. I would like to thank all my coaches, trainers, models and mentors for giving me the inspiration to making The Power of Life Mastery a success. You have given me more than I could ever imagine giving you back.

I would also like to thank the thousands of clients that I've seen over the past few years. I've learned the most valuable lessons from each and every single one of you.

I would also like to express my gratitude to all the people involved in my life. The people from my past, in my present, and the ones to come into my future will continue to inspire me and help me inspire millions.

And last but not least, I would like to thank my family and friends for believing in me and in the absolute power of life mastery.

CONTENTS

INTRODUCTION

What would your life be like if you knew that nothing could hold you back? If you were absolutely sure that you could accomplish anything you set out to do, how would things be different? I will demonstrate to you in the next several pages that you are, in fact, capable of having, doing, being and achieving whatever you wish. These claims are not based on a hunch or some unrealistic form of positive thinking. I will give you solid proof, backed by science, which confirms you are much more powerful than you ever imagined. This book contains a step by-step-guide to creating positive lasting changes in any area of your life. These pages are a blueprint that will lead you to your own positive, personal transformation.

By reading this now you have already started to write a new chapter of your personal story. You are about to embark on a journey, one that will continue to reward you for a lifetime. Technology has now proved to be true what philosophers have been saying for thousands of years: we are what we think, we do create our own destinies, and the possibilities in life are virtually endless.

Throughout the entire history of this planet, there has never been anyone exactly like you, and there will never be another once you're gone. You are an individual, which means that you are unique, one of a kind. No one can do what you can do exactly the way that you can do it. In short, you have a very special place in this universe. You will create on this earth something that wasn't here before you came. Only you can bring forth the good that is yours—that knowledge, that understanding, that special gift which took form the precise moment that you were born. Nobody is going to write your book, produce your play or sing your song. No one else will touch the hearts of those people that only you can reach. Nobody is going to bring your "good" into the world. It's yours, and without you, this world cannot truly become its best.

I'd like you to just take a moment and consider what could happen if you removed self-doubt, fear and procrastination from your life. What would things be like if you felt free to allow what is inside you to come out into the world? You'll find in this book the keys to unlocking your potential—the secrets to leading a life full of joy, satisfaction and personal fulfillment. As you continue to read and perform the included exercises, you will discover a path that leads to your true life's purpose. You will encounter obstacles along the way—make no mistake of that. Yet, the challenges that you encounter will only serve to make you stronger and more capable of achieving your goals.

You are writing your own story. You are the director, star and producer of your life. Other people may have influenced the way things have unfolded up until now. The next page of your script, however, has yet to be written. The second half of your story is yours alone to create.

PART I: MINDSET

CHAPTER I

What Do You Really Want?

Though you may have heard what I'm about to tell you many times before, it's crucial to your journey to personal fulfillment: the first step to achieving any goal is getting a clear picture of what it is you want. After all, you can't expect to get anywhere in life if you don't know where you want to go. As the saying goes, "If you don't know where you're going, then any road will take you there."

People without direction simply float through life aimlessly. They often start one project after another, but never finish. They dream and fantasize about improving their circumstances while staying in the same place, year after year. They say they want to have more, but never really define what "more" means—a grave and critical mistake. It's no wonder that only a few people end up getting what they really want out of life.

If, in any area of your life, you want something different from what you have right now, you need to become incredibly clear about your goals. Achieving clarity is like bringing a camera lens into focus. When the image that you are looking at is blurry, it's almost impossible to discern the best angle of approach. The best you can do is randomly take pictures and hope you get something of value in the end. The problem with this strategy is that you can spend all day taking photos and then return home to discover that none of them are worthwhile.

When you start thinking about your goals in a precise manner, your brain turns into something like a homing mechanism. You become aware of, find, and attract those things that will help you get to your target location. A part of your brain called the reticular activating system, RAS, actually decides what comes into your awareness. Have you ever bought a new outfit and later noticed many people around you wearing the same thing or something similar? Did you ever buy a new car, only to later see the same model everywhere you went? Think about when you're in a crowded room where everybody is talking and all the voices blend into a sort of background noise. Despite that "blending," if someone suddenly called your name, your brain would pick it up automatically.

In all of these cases, your reticular activating system was working for you. That same car or outfit was around you the whole time, but your decision to purchase it told your brain that the item was of importance. The same thing happens when there's a lot of noise and someone calls your name. Your brain is built to ignore about ninety-nine percent of everything that goes on in your environment. It only allows you to notice those things that have value to you. It does so to keep you from being overwhelmed by the thousands of things going on around you at any given moment. This is why it's so important to be specific when it comes to setting your goals. It takes a clear mental picture to put your reticular activating system in motion, drawing your attention to those things that can help you succeed.

The first thing you want to do is create a sharp mental image of your desired outcome. Don't try to rush or move too quickly through the process of clarifying your goals, as this may be your most important step in paving your way to personal achievement. If you want to earn more money, decide exactly how much you wish to make. Think of a specific number—what you'd like to produce each week, each month, each year. If you want a better relationship, then determine what "better" would look like to you. How would you and your ideal mate talk to, relate to, and act toward one another? If you want to travel, where exactly do you wish to go? What exactly will you do when you get there? Put as much detail as you can into the image of your ideal future. Doing this will give you a sense of direction and even help you feel more confident about reaching your goals. Undefined challenges often seem insurmountable. When a problem is defined, however, it becomes real and therefore has a real solution.

So take a few moments to think about what you really want to achieve. What do you want out of a relationship? What do you want out of a career in terms of financial goals and personal achievements? What do you wish you could give back to society? The more you think about this, the more detailed that image of your life will become.

Here's an example of what I mean. Let's say that you currently live in a very cold climate, and you're really uncomfortable there. You are totally fed up with scraping ice from your car in the morning, trudging through snow, and having to face freezing temperatures every day. Let's also say that you own a sailboat, and one day you decide that you're ready to leave. You really want to go someplace warmer, perhaps a tropical climate. So you take your boat out to the ocean and set sail. You aren't concerned with exactly where you'll go. You just take off and hope that your future destination is better than the place you're leaving.

You probably know, as an outsider thinking about this scenario, that your chances of finding the right type of environment this way would be slim to none. You would likely end up somewhere that seems bad to you—or even worse than your previous home. In fact, you may wander around the ocean for eternity without ever setting foot on solid ground. This is to say that, in order to achieve a certain outcome, you must have the end result firmly in mind.

This is also true when it comes to navigating your life. When you have a clear mental picture of your "destination"—the product you want from your life—that image acts as a compass that continuously steers you in the right direction. When you don't have your destination in focus, however, the storms of life can knock you right off track and you will likely end up going nowhere fast.

Before you decide where to go, however, you have to know exactly where you are right now. When you book an airline flight, you need to provide both your intended destination and city of departure. Being aware of your life's current conditions is just as important as determining how you want them to change. Without a clear and current assessment of your present circumstances, you won't know what in your life needs to be adjusted or improved.

Examine the different areas of your life, specifically those that you want to change, and ask yourself, "What is this part of my life like right now?" It's important to be brutally honest with yourself at this point. If you want to be healthier, but you're about thirty pounds overweight, eat junk food on a regular basis, and get no exercise whatsoever, then tell yourself that. Trying to sugarcoat the way things have been going or pretending they are better than they are will only hurt you in the end.

On the following pages, you can fill in information regarding the nature of your goals. This worksheet will help you to first define the existing condition of any area of your life, and then create a clear representation of your desired outcome. Spend as much time as you need to complete these pages and go into real detail about what you really want. The more you write down, the more refined your picture of success will become.

CHAPTER I:

WORKSHEET

Financial Goals

Describe the current state of your finances.

How have you been producing these results until now?

What things should you do more of to have a greater positive impact on your income?

What habits should you eliminate or lessen?

How much money do you want to earn?

Over what time frame do you want to achieve this?

When you have reached your financial goal, what will you have, do or experience that you don't right now?

What can you do today/this week/this month that will move you closer to your financial goal?

Physical Goals

What is the state of your health right now?

In what ways could you be healthier or fitter?

What habits have been holding you back from achieving your fitness goals?

What kind of rituals or habits could you adopt that would significantly improve the quality of your health?

Relationship Goals

How do you want to project yourself to other people? (What kind of person do you want people to see you as?)

What qualities do you need to develop or strengthen to become that type of person?

What kind of people do you need to surround yourself with to support your personal transformation?

Which of your habits are inhibiting your personal growth?

Over the next year, is it your intention to stay single, start dating, get married or strengthen your current relationship?

Describe your ideal mate.

Attitude Goals

What is the general attitude that you've been carrying with you through life?

How do you typically feel for most of the day?

What beliefs have been holding you back from becoming more successful?

To become the type of person who has what you want, how would you need to change your attitude?

Enjoyment Goals

What type of things do you really enjoy doing?

What could you do to make room in your life for more of that?

List some activities you can choose from each day to get more enjoyment out of life.

Contribution Goals

What kinds of things can you do to contribute or give back to your community, society or world at large?

What will you do this week to make a positive impact on someone else?

CHAPTER II

~~Believe~~ Know You Can Do It

I understand the excitement you must be experiencing as you read this book. I also understand that you're eager to start changing your life to make it more fulfilling. However, if you haven't done the previous assignment, please stop reading now and go back to doing it. Remember, the main chapter of your life now is rewriting your future, and the first milestone is writing clear and compelling goals. Go back, finish the assignment to your highest level of satisfaction, and then come back to continue this journey with me. I'll be right here waiting for you.

Now you have a clear vision of what you really want. You have a clear picture of your goals firmly in mind. You know what success looks like inside and out. Next, you must know, deep in your heart, that you can accomplish what you are setting out to achieve—that attaining this goal is possible for you. There's a big difference between believing something and knowing it. To be able to turn your dreams into reality, you must go beyond belief and into "knowing."

When you believe something, deep down inside you understand that your belief might not be true—otherwise, it would be a fact, not a belief. When you believe that you can have something, you know there's a possibility of not getting it. You may believe your term paper is the best one, but you know that the teacher may not necessarily share your opinion. You may believe you deserve to get that promotion, but you also know there's a chance it might not happen.

When you know something, however, you mentally cut off the possibility of it being not true. There's no doubt in "knowing." You know when you wake up in the morning that the floor beneath you is solid. You wouldn't get out of bed otherwise. If you squeeze a lemon, you know lemon juice is going to come out. There is no possibility that it might end up being grape or orange.

When it comes to the matter of achieving your goals, you have to get into the business of knowing. Know that other people have achieved enormous success and they were no better, more capable or smarter than you are. Know that you are a special and exceptional person, capable of doing, having and being more than you have given yourself credit for in the past.

Getting past believing that you can do something and entering the realm of knowing it means feeling the truth of what you affirm in every fiber of your being. We live in the information age, where technology makes it possible for people to acquire information at the touch of a button. However, there's a saying, "If information was all we needed, then everyone would be healthy, rich and happy." There is a significant difference between knowing what to do and actually doing it. Most people who want to lose weight have learned every weight loss and fitness technique that exists. However, they've never actually made the distinction between "losing weight" and "getting rid of excess weight." Losing means some kind of pain. We lose things we like, things we love, and things we've grown emotionally dependent on. Once we understand that there is no actual losing in weight loss, we can create enough drive and motivation in our minds to force us to take massive action. Many people who want financial success have studied material from some of the greatest financial producers in history, yet they've never achieved financial freedom.

Only *applied* information—not information alone—can truly produce the results that we want. The key is not simply learning more; it is discovering how to get ourselves motivated enough to take action.

Motivation inspires action, which in turn breeds momentum. Momentum is a powerful driving force that will help you achieve whatever it is that you want. If you want to gain momentum, you need to trust in the process. Let's say that you want to get rid of excess weight. You wouldn't just cut down on your caloric intake, start exercising for one day and then say, "Well, that's it. I've done it. I'll get thinner from here on out." You know that it takes consistent effort to get from your current fitness level to where you want to be. Isn't the same thing true in life? When you do the right things, somewhere inside you know that your efforts will eventually lead to progress. You have to trust in the process, knowing that what you do each day will eventually accumulate into a desired result. You must know that this is true. Anything less than absolute certainty will not guide you to do what's needed in pursuit of your goals. Instead, you will end up drifting down the road of delusion.

The first part of this step is recognizing the possibilities that are out there for you. Do you think you don't have the money it takes to achieve your goals? Stories of poverty-stricken people who achieve massive success are almost commonplace. Do you feel as if you don't have the resources, intelligence or contacts to pursue your dream? Look around and I'll bet you will find countless others who started with less than you who have, yet accomplished similar aspirations.

Life rarely unfolds in a straight line. Read biographies of people who have become successful in your chosen field. What you will find is that these people had to overcome all sorts of challenges on the way to achieving their dreams. Often we assume that those who've made it have walked the straight path to success. You see a star or a popular sports figure on TV, for instance, and it seems like this person can do no wrong. What you don't see are the 20,000 hours of practice that your favorite athlete put in before he became a household name. You don't hear about the hundreds of auditions that your favorite actor or actress failed before getting his or her big break.

When we look at performers in our current culture, we see only a finished product. People believe that those in the spotlight are perfect and have not faced the difficulties that most of us have. Nothing could be further from the truth. People do not come out of the womb slam dunking a basketball, writing great plays or producing wonderful musicals. Genius is rarely born and mostly created. These skills are developed through time, dedication, determination and patience. Others have developed the skills that you want; therefore, you too can achieve greatness. The so-called "stars" of any industry are people who have had a deep passion for what they do. Their passion inspired action, which produced a momentum that led to enormous success.

You can genuinely turn your belief into a "knowing." What you seek is not as farfetched as you may think. You were born with everything you need to get what you want out of life. Our biggest challenges are not those that we face on the way to our goals; they are the ones we invent for ourselves when we lack confidence in our own power to achieve those goals.

Certain types of public exhibitions, known as flea circuses, were once widely popular. These were novelty shows, in which "trainers" would bring fleas to perform various physical acts. People prevented their fleas from escaping the arena in a very interesting way. Between shows, the fleas were kept in a glass container, the lid of which was set below the fleas' normal jumping range. At first, the fleas would slam their heads against the unusually low top. But they would eventually adjust their leap to a level that was just below the new limitation. Over time, the lid was lowered little by little, and consequently, the fleas kept modifying their jumping height to match the newest restrictions. When the lid was finally removed, the fleas would only jump to the height that they had been conditioned to. Though nothing was stopping them from getting out of the container, the fleas would continue to respect the limit they believed was there.

People do the same thing in everyday life. Someone may believe that making the kind of money that he wants is just not realistic, but this belief may simply come from the observation that no one he knows has ever done it before. That's not a genuine reason to believe anything. Other people are not you, so their lack of success should have nothing to do with what you plan to achieve. Another person may believe that a person of her gender just couldn't make it within a certain field of industry. Again, this belief is probably the product of imaginary limitations. In fact, much of the pain you experience has resulted from accepting false beliefs during some time in your life.

We all play roles in life. You can play the role of victim or martyr. You can play the role of someone who is passionate about life, or one who simply goes through the motions. You can also play the role of someone who achieves massive success in any environment. However, the important thing to remember is that you get to choose. You can make a decision to switch characters and change direction at any time. It's all up to you. Life doesn't really care which role you take on. It will support you as whatever character you choose to be. If you choose to play the role of being broke, life will support you. It has no knowledge of your family's needs or financial obligations. If your character is one who always gets taken advantage of, life will support you in this role as well. Life won't consider the fact that you are kindhearted and humble.

Famed American author Napoleon Hill once said, "There are no limitations to the mind except those we acknowledge." So you have to break through the ceiling of your perceived limits. Knowing that you can do what's needed is one of the biggest accomplishments you can achieve on your way to success.

Remember that your belief systems, values and habitual routines are stored at the subconscious level of mind. They operate outside of your normal awareness. You must do some solid detective work to uncover the beliefs that are hurting you; you can't change anything that you don't know is there. More importantly, how do you adjust your beliefs and values so that they naturally align with your goals? How do you, in essence, set goals at the subconscious level, so that your mind does the dirty work of pushing you past perceived barriers? In order to deliberately achieve something new, you must be able to see yourself having it. The tricky thing is that because we'll often view a goal as something that we are seeking to achieve, the subconscious will become locked in this perpetual state of *going* for what you want, instead of *having it*. I cannot stress this point enough.

Before you set out to achieve any goal, you must see yourself in the final picture first, as if you've already achieved it. Then, your subconscious will do whatever is necessary to guide you through the appropriate action steps. This is what's known as "Starting with the end in mind." When you do it correctly, your mind will design the perfect plan to lead you to that end result.

Most people do exactly the opposite, however. They continuously picture how overweight they are, while "wanting" to get rid of that extra 50 pounds. They "want" to earn more money, but remain focused on an empty bank account. They imagine how awkward they are with the opposite sex, while trying to establish a loving and compassionate relationship. This doesn't work, because human beings are goal-seeking creatures driven by emotions. Emotions are what drive behavior, and our subconscious minds are always striving to make our dominant thoughts become reality. Therefore, you must teach yourself to feel good about your goals, as though what you want is already in your possession. Doing this will also help you plot out a course that will lead you to achieving your goals. Sometimes when you've created a sizable goal, it can be difficult to figure out the first steps you should take, but when you mentally step into that final picture, you can look back and think of what it took to get you there. This is a very clever way to get your mind moving in the right direction.

Let me give you an example. You may find it useful to create a timeline on a blank sheet of paper as I run you through it. Say you want to raise 15,000 dollars for a new car in six months. So you get into the end result of that goal. You've practiced seeing, hearing and feeling what it would be like to have that car and you absorb that on every level. What you could do, from that final position, is look back and say, "Where was I thirty days ago, at the end of my fifth month?" What did it take to get from there to here? You can then break those steps down further, into weekly and even daily goals.

Next, go to that place where you would be at the end of five months. In order to be there, where would you have had to have been thirty days before that, at the end of your fourth month? What did it take? What did you need to do to get from the fourth to the fifth month? Again, break down those steps. Keep going back through time until you know exactly what you need to do, from today onward, to reach the next milestone. Now you have a well-orchestrated plan for getting that new car, with clear and specific daily tasks that will bring you closer to your goal.

Problems will also arise, however, if your conscious and subconscious are not in agreement. This happens when your conscious mind wants one thing, but the subconscious mind holds on to a belief that keeps you from getting it. It's like when a person who wants to find a better relationship also has a deep-seated fear of intimacy. Or what if an individual wants to become wealthy but was taught as a child that only evil people make lots of money? You may have been trained to believe some things early on that will get in the way of what you want right now. So you must get aligned, meaning you need to get both your conscious and subconscious minds pointed in the same direction.

One way to make this happen is to practice holding on to your goal at the level of "being." This means that if you want to write a book, start thinking of yourself as being an author. If you want to start your own business, start thinking of yourself as being an entrepreneur. If you want to attend culinary school, start thinking of yourself as being a chef. The important thing is to conceptualize, feel and experience your goal as being a new "identity" for yourself. See, it's less about what you want to achieve and more about who you need to become.

Next are some exercises that you can perform to really establish a deep sense of knowing that you can do what you want. Again, take time to fill out the following forms completely. Do the exercises knowing that if you follow the process, you truly can and will achieve your goals.

CHAPTER II:

WORKSHEET

Who can you think of who has achieved the same results that you want?

What have those people been doing that you're not doing now?

How can you improve your practice or performance to align your efforts with those of people who have become successful in this field?

Think of those people who have achieved massive success in your chosen field. Find a biography of one of these individuals and read it through. Note, here, what you have learned.

What limiting beliefs have you been holding on to that may have held you back from success in the past?

CHAPTER III

Know That You Deserve It

After knowing that you can achieve your goals, you must also know that you deserve to do so. All human beings have what is known as a "self image." This is an internal assessment of a person's own abilities, worth and value. This image controls what you will tend to think, feel and do in any area of life. This is important to remember because a person will never outperform his or her own self image.

If you truly believe that you're a shy person, then you will act "shyly" whenever an opportunity to communicate comes your way. You will always stay consistent with how you see yourself on the inside, even though circumstances may call for you to act differently. If you consider yourself to be a fit and healthy person who rarely gets sick, then you'll continue to do things that support that image of who you know yourself to be. You'll go for morning jogs, eat healthy foods, and take care of your body in other ways, all because you see yourself as someone who takes pride in his or her health.

Similarly, if you see yourself as someone who's chronically sick—if you always think that illness is waiting just around the corner—you will act in ways that help you become ill on a regular basis. We've all known people like this, those who seem to attract illness wherever they go. Others, however, seem to be the picture of perfect health and go for many years without contracting as much as a common cold.

All of this comes as a result of what we expect out of life. We tend to manifest and prove true our deepest beliefs. If you don't agree, I invite you to challenge me on this one, and just take a quick look at your life. What you are producing now, in any area, is a direct reflection of some internal belief you have about that part of your life, is it not?

Interestingly, many of our beliefs, especially those that seem to hold us back the most, are often subconscious. We didn't choose them, but simply picked them up from parents, peers and members of the community. A limiting belief can wreak such havoc on your life because you probably don't even know it exists. It hides beneath the surface of your personality, causing you to act out in many ways that don't serve you. The good news, though, is that this limiting belief is not a solid knowledge. This means that, together, we can mold it, shape it, and reframe it into the kind of empowering knowledge that you need to achieve more health, wealth and happiness.

If you never seem to have enough money, it is because you have a belief that stops you from producing wealth. Perhaps you grew up in a financially challenged family, and a part of your mind became convinced that there would just never be enough. Maybe you felt frustrated with your parents because they were tight with money, and you never got to spend a dime on recreation. Even though you may be all grown up today, you may find yourself spending like crazy just to gain that sense of freedom, certainty and significance that you once felt deprived of. If you find yourself sabotaging one relationship after another, part of your mind retains a negative belief about romantic partnerships. You may have felt abandoned by a certain parent as a child and now find it hard to trust other people. You may have been hurt by someone dear to you and, on some level, decided that you would never allow yourself to be vulnerable again. Whatever the story may be, our beliefs play a major role in shaping the quality of our lives. If you believe that you cannot do something, you won't put forth the effort it takes to make things happen. This is especially true when it comes to your belief about what you deserve out of life. You will never let yourself have more than you think you deserve. You may say, "Of course I deserve more. I'm not going to stand in my own way; that would be silly." However, belief systems are stored in the subconscious level of your mind. They operate below your awareness while guiding your thoughts, feelings and actions from behind the scenes.

So part of knowing that you deserve more involves rooting out those limiting beliefs and replacing them with ones that better serve your ambitions. You then want to transform those new beliefs into a solid sense of knowing that you deserve more. Remember that beliefs are just opinions, not facts. Considering that, doesn't it stand to reason that you should only hold on to those that can give you a positive outcome? Well, in order to do that, you need to become your own biggest cheerleader, the one who stands up for your dreams against all opposition. To facilitate becoming this person, you must feel worthy of having that which you wish to create. How you feel about yourself has a huge impact on how far you go. In the long run, you can only live up (or down) to your own expectations. Though you can kind of ride on someone else's belief in you for a short while, you cannot go far without developing a sense of faith in your own abilities. No one can really make you feel good about yourself. It's is all up to you.

You probably wouldn't go above and beyond the call of duty to help someone get something you really didn't think he or she deserved. The same is true when it comes to your own life. This is why it is paramount that you learn to like yourself—and there's a lot to like! When you begin to appreciate your own inner value, it will come through in everything that you do. You'll make more of an effort and get more focused on the fact that what you want can become a reality. The more you like yourself—the more you think of yourself as someone who has value—the more you can open yourself up to opportunities that come your way. You'll feel better, go after bigger goals and go through challenges without getting discouraged.

On the other hand, a person who doesn't feel worthy will not have a self-image that allows him or her to enjoy good fortune. That person will always be expecting things in the world to fall apart. If you don't believe yourself to be worthy of something, you will likely feel guilty about having it. You may even subconsciously sabotage yourself and find that you just can't seem to hold on to anything good.

Success happens from the inside-out. You have to work on resolving some of your own internal barriers before things will change in the environment. If you want more out of life, then the first step is to convince yourself that you deserve it. We really do create our own destinies. We cannot see past what we believe to be true. Our beliefs are then turned into reality, at least through the lenses of our own individual perceptions. We manifest our subconscious beliefs, those things that we really hold as truths, despite what we tell others and ourselves. If you believe, on a deep level, that you're a loser, then you simply won't do what it takes to win. Each of your beliefs, to you, is a certainty, just like the law of gravity. You wouldn't leap from the top of a twenty-story building without a parachute because you would be certain that there was a very slim chance of survival. Similarly, your subconscious mind perceives the act of going against one of your deeply held beliefs as a life-threatening issue.

Many of your automatic emotional reactions come from this primitive part of your awareness. This area of your mind is primarily concerned with your survival—and it considers your physical and emotional survival to be of equal importance. It creates all sorts of defense mechanisms to give you a sense of security about yourself and the world around you.

The truth is that reinforcing your limiting beliefs actually feels good on some level. We like to feel like we're right, like we're certain about our limited interpretations. However, it doesn't make sense to give up true happiness and fulfillment in exchange for a sense of certainty. Doing this does not serve your ambitions in any way. In order to create powerful, personal change in any area of your life, you must become unwilling to avoid the truth. You must refuse to blame others for your circumstances and take responsibility for producing better outcomes. Blame is a futile practice that distorts the thinking of whoever is finding fault. You must pursue a deeper reality, one that lies beneath the stories that you have become accustomed to creating.

The truth will reveal itself to you when you are prepared to find it. As long as you hold on to egotistical needs—to be right, in control and unaccountable—you won't make the progress necessary to get to your goal. Achieving anything worthwhile is really a feat of self-development, of moving away from a false persona and toward who it is that you really are.

Your thoughts are powerful. When you project certain attitudes and ideas on a consistent basis, those thoughts start to become physical reality. Just think about this for a second. Your life could have unfolded in a number of different ways. You made decisions in the past, and those choices led you to encounter certain outcomes. Your choices have always been selected from among those that you perceived to be available to you, but the possibility of creating many *more* realities also existed all along. You could say that these alternate versions of your life exist simultaneously. You simply narrowed your focus to include only those circumstances that matched the habitual thought patterns and beliefs you had acquired.

All you have to do is expand your awareness to realize that you have the power to bring another world for yourself into being, one in which you are living the life of your dreams. Your ability to create is virtually unlimited. All that you have to do is know that what you want is possible, know you deserve it and decide to make it happen. However, you have to plug in to that enormous reservoir of energy at your disposal.

You can never receive more than you are capable of managing at any time. The universe is like an unlimited well of resources. If it were an actual well, how much water could you take from it? You may say, "As much as I want," but that's not necessarily true. The amount that you could receive would depend on your awareness of the well, the size of your container and your ability to carry it. If you believed that the well only contained a very small amount of water, you may not even make the journey to find it. If you knew of the well's magnitude, but only had a tiny little cup in your possession, that knowledge wouldn't do you much good. If you were aware of the well and had a fairly large container, you would still have to be able to carry however much you took. Your understanding of the unlimited power that you have to create is analogous to your knowledge of the well. Your knowledge of your command over this power is comparable to the size of your container. Finally, the mindset development portion of your self-improvement program will determine your ability to carry whatever you take. Does that make sense?

You must not only want to do better, but also know that you deserve it. Some people feel guilty about the idea of wanting more. They say, "So many people in the world are doing badly. Who am I to achieve my dreams and goals?" However, this kind of thinking is completely backwards. It doesn't do those who are suffering any good for you to be down in the dumps with them. On the other hand, if you start making things happen for yourself, you'll soon have the resources and ability to help others who haven't made it yet. You won't be able to help anyone until you help yourself first, though. You can't give anything to another person that you, yourself, don't possess. This means that it is your duty to do what you can to attain a higher quality of life. If you won't do it for yourself, then do it for the countless other people who could benefit from it.

Some people, however, find it hard to feel deserving of the good that comes their way. Maybe you'll even find yourself relating to some of the following examples. A person might walk around in ragged shoes, not because he doesn't have the money for new ones, but because he just feels too uncomfortable about spending a few extra dollars on himself. Someone else might find herself barely scraping by, month after month, just because she has never given herself permission to do better. Then there are those who show up to work, doing just enough to collect a paycheck, when they have so much untapped potential.

Over the past few years, I've been privileged and honored to have coached a vast array of people to reach their peak performance. From politicians, business pioneers, celebrities and high profile clients who earn six- to seven-figure incomes a month, to average

Joes and clients who barely have enough to scrape by. Regardless of people's socioeconomic status, the psychological laws of peak performance apply to everyone equally. When you're going for your dreams, seventy, eighty or even ninety percent won't cut it! Getting what you want out of life is like climbing to the top of a mountain. Either you do, or you don't. There is no in-between. No one remembers who made it halfway up Mount Everest. Some attempters were briefly celebrated for being the first to go so far at the time, but only those who've reached the peak are able to grace the Wall of Fame.

This is not to say that it isn't an accomplishment to explore uncharted areas of achievement, but you have your own milestones to reach, your own personal peak, which continues rising higher and higher. Never allow yourself to settle for less. You know many people in the world today are just settling—for jobs they don't want, relationships they aren't happy with, and bodies they don't feel good about—all because they don't think they deserve better or have the power to do anything about it. You do deserve the very best—not the average, the simple or the easy, but the absolute best. You have no idea of how long you'll be on his planet. You don't know how fast your window of opportunity is closing. So it is essential that you get absolutely everything you can out of life in every moment.

What would you do if you knew that you couldn't fail? What would you do if you could achieve anything at all, money was no object, and you had access to all the resources you needed? The answer to that question will likely identify the top of your mountain. See, most of us think about that ultimate goal and focus only on the risks involved. Instead, you could be using that energy to design a series of action steps that will get you there. Sometimes, you can get so used to settling for less that, after a while, it doesn't seem that bad. I know a guy who remained in an extremely toxic relationship for more than ten years. When I asked how he could go through all that for so long, he replied, "Over time, that just became my normal reality." As silly as that sounds, many of us go through the same experience in different areas of life. You might get used to holding that mediocre position at work for so long that you don't even notice opportunities passing you by. You may have been living from check-to-check for so long that you can't even picture yourself climbing out of that financial hole. When you become accustomed to settling for less, you start becoming afraid to succeed. And that's definitely not a place that you want to be in. You must, and I mean MUST, get comfortable with the fact that you can have whatever you want, as long as you are willing to go for it, accept it and know that you deserve it.

If you did know this, in the deepest levels of your being, what kind of difference would that make for you? What would you be, do, and produce if you were willing to put yourself out there? Instead of focusing on how hard something's going to be, think about why you're doing it. Remember that a big enough "WHY" can move mountains.

I'm going to walk you through a simple process that will enable you to uncover and replace any limiting beliefs you may have about deserving your dream. In performing this exercise, you will also learn to truly know that you can have, do and be whatever you want. Again, take all the time you need to complete this exercise. This process is essential to your growth and development.

CHAPTER III:

WORKSHEET

Do you ever get the feeling that you're not worthy of achieving certain goals?

Do you ever feel like your ability to live up to others' expectations determines your value?

Do you tend to procrastinate?

When you put off doing an important task, do you believe deep down inside that you wouldn't be able to carry it out successfully?

Do you ever believe that you have something important, valuable and appropriate to say, yet still refrain from speaking up?

As a child, were you encouraged to pursue your personal goals?

Were you supported in individual pursuits, even if they were quite different from those of your parents?

Have you ever worried that failing at a particular task would mean that you'd never be able to succeed in the future?

Did influential people in your life ever shout at or criticize you harshly for making a mistake?

What are some things you heard early in life that could be negatively affecting your ability to achieve right now?

CHAPTER III:

Bonus Exercise

Think about the things you've written down. Consider whether any of these events left you feeling as though you weren't worthy of achieving your goals. This bonus exercise will do miracles for you if you allow yourself to let your imagination run wild. As you read this exercise, I suggest you create very vivid images in your head and make your memories as alive as possible. It may be useful to read it a few times before you get the general notion of it. After you have a clear idea about what you need to do, close your eyes and visualize those scenes, making them as real and as honest as possible.

Now, imagine that you're sitting in front of a small television. On it, you can see another child going through the same events that you described earlier. As you watch each scene, consider whether there could be other interpretations of the adult's behavior. Perhaps the mother, father, or whoever was involved was just upset with the child for not doing what they wanted right then. Maybe they weren't making any kind of judgment about whether the child was worthy or not. Perhaps the adult figure was simply wrong about the child's ability or potential. Human beings are not perfect and are often mistaken about their judgments of other people. The adults in those scenes are no different. Maybe the adults involved held impractical beliefs about how the child should have acted. Children are inexperienced. People don't learn to be good at a lot of things until they become older. It's just a natural part of growing up. Perhaps the adults were attempting to implement some type of reverse psychology, thinking that challenging the child in this way would make him or her work harder.

You can see that there are many alternative interpretations of the same event. These other interpretations often fit the situation just as well as the one reached by the child involved. Do you see how the child's self-evaluation of being undeserving was just an opinion and not a fact? Would you go to a child of that age now and ask him or her to interpret the events of your life for you? The events that you experienced could have had a number of different and, equally as valid, meanings. However, the child interpreted each event in the same way, as proof that he or she wasn't worthy, deserving or good enough.

When you give an event meaning, you then perceive that meaning each time a similar occasion comes about. This leads to a belief that the way you have interpreted these events is real, when it's really not. It is only the product of a very young mind, a mind that does not yet have the ability to evaluate complex interactions. Whatever you say to yourself when an event occurs is the meaning you assign to it in your mind. You didn't really learn anything about your life through these experiences. You simply felt, inside, that you weren't good enough.

Imagine that you are a child again, only now you have the ability to perceive the alternative interpretations of those life events. When parents or authority figures become angry, you can now see that you have a choice in deciding what that means. Now, intentionally give those scenes another meaning. Notice what it feels like to interpret these events in a different way. Knowing what you know now, do you still feel as though you were unworthy or undeserving of having what you want? Your feelings were caused by interpretation, not reality. Do you see now that the thought of not being worthy was never a fact? Take a deep breath, exhale and allow this new understanding to seep into every part of your being. Notice how the thought of not being good enough no longer has the same meaning to you that it once did. If you had someone to walk you through this process when you were younger, would you have established the same beliefs as you did before? How would have your life turned out differently? Once you answer these questions, you can move on to the next step of achieving your dreams.

CHAPTER IV

Commit Yourself to the Process

By now, we both know that it's essential to have clear and well-defined goals. However, just setting a goal is not enough to make powerful changes happen. Success is a process, a journey of sorts. Moving toward your goal-making progress day-by-day defines your level of success. So, one of the things that you must do is commit yourself to the process involved in getting what you want.

Let's say that you typically run a mile in twelve minutes, and your goal is to do it in six. The day after setting this goal, you wouldn't be able to just go out and cut your running time in half. You know there's a preparation process, things you must do to become capable of accomplishing your chosen task. You might start out by "picking-up" your pace and improving your stride. You may practice breathing differently or running harder at certain parts of the distance. Over several weeks, you'd probably go from finishing the mile in twelve minutes, to running it in eleven, ten, nine and so on. However, that progress is where the real "juice" is. It's getting those increasingly positive results that build up the feeling of being successful. Had you accomplished what you wanted to in one day, doing so might not have held much meaning for you. Many people have accomplished big things, only to feel disappointed in the end. They say to themselves, "Is that it? Is that all there is? What do I do now?" The real value of going after your goals is not in what you achieve, but who you become in the process. Focus on becoming the right person and the goal will take care of itself.

In order to become the right person, you must commit yourself to the process. Running that six-minute mile could only take place as a result of doing certain things consistently. You'd have to put in a considerable amount of specialized training over a period of time before you would see any results. You would have to devote yourself to doing things every day that enabled you to develop the lifestyle changes that would get you to where you wanted to go. You would not expect to reach your target weight after just one day of exercise. Likewise, your goal won't magically become a reality the very moment that you begin to take action.

Think of success as something you must nurture and grow, like a seed planted in the ground. You don't plant a seed, throw some water on it and plan on seeing results in the same day. You *know* that every plant takes a certain amount of time to go from seed to sprout. The same is true when it comes to creating new things in your life. You must nurture the seeds of your dreams for a certain amount of time before they take root and mature. A farmer may have to spend months caring for a fruit tree before its branches produce anything of value. However, the farmer knows that if he puts the seed in fertile soil, gives it a certain amount of water each day, exposes it to sunlight and offers the proper nutrients, eventually fruit will come. He simply has to create the proper conditions for success, and what he wants will naturally come to pass.

When pursuing your goals, you have to know that success will come when you make a habit of doing the right things. Every action is a cause that has an effect. Everything that you do has a natural consequence. What you have in your life today has resulted from what you did yesterday, last week, last month and last year. What you will have tomorrow, next week, next month and next year is being created by what you do right now. So it's essential that you dedicate yourself to the process of success right now.

A great tennis player doesn't just show up one day and play an outstanding game. In the months leading up to a match, she does lots of little things that make a big difference. She learns how to turn her wrist, ever so slightly, in order to get the ball to land in that perfect spot. She works on getting to the ball that would have gone out of bounds by moving her feet just a little bit quicker. She works on all of these small things every single day, making the type of progress that begins in inches and ends up as miles. What you see on TV is just the end result, the natural consequence of doing little things well every day. So what I'm asking you to do is dedicate yourself to performing those things that will help you achieve your goal on a consistent basis.

We create our lives through habits. In any area of your life, what you have right now is the natural effect of the routines that you've been following up to this point. If you never get enough sleep and eat nothing but junk food, you're going to feel an unnatural loss of energy each day. If you want your circumstances to change, you're going to have to make an adjustment in your routine.

If you want to create monetary wealth, then study the habits of people who are earning the income you'd like to have. Notice what they're doing consistently that you're not. Incorporate these behaviors into your daily routine. This process is called "modeling" and it works extremely well. You have to stick with it, though. You must have faith in the process, knowing that if you develop the habits of successful people you too will achieve greatness.

If you want to get rid of that extra weight or become healthier, take a look at people who are now performing at your desired fitness level. Chances are that they aren't rolling out of bed at noon, skipping breakfast and downing a large soda while watching hours of TV. If you want to get out of an old rut and into a better quality of life, you're going to have to raise the bar on the quality of your habits and commit yourself to those standards every single day.

When you know that the process works, you won't be quick to give up as soon as hard times come your way. Reaching for your goal is like building a house. In the first stages of construction, a house looks like no more than a slab of concrete, littered about with pieces of metal and lumber. Little by little, however, it begins to take form. Masons begin laying bricks along the outside walls. Carpenters come in and create a framework for the interior dividers. Electricians show up and run wiring throughout the entire structure. Roofers top the house off with a tightly sealed ceiling. After a little paint and landscaping, what you'll see is a beautiful structure fit to meet the needs of its future occupants. A house can be put together in this way because the builders have a process that works. They don't lose hope in the beginning. They don't despair when what they've made so far looks crude and unfinished. Every standing house today was once just a blueprint—a goal, if you will. It only exists because several people were once willing to have faith in the process. Can you see how this metaphor mirrors the story of your life? If you decide to improve your monetary situation and don't see a dramatic change in the first two weeks, don't worry. You may have spent the last several years digging yourself into a financial hole. It's going to take time for you to reach a balance point that allows you to make a visible impact on your financial goals.

People probably won't line up at your door the moment that you decide to be more outgoing and make new friends. You may have spent the last several years behaving in a timid and withdrawn manner. You will need to learn new ways of communicating and practice them in order to become more effective interacting with people.

When you know what you should do, and you do it consistently, success is inevitable. The only way you can fail is if you give up before reaching your goal. The process also cleanses you of those aspects of personality that you no longer need to hold on to. If you start getting up early every morning to work out, you're going to develop more than a healthier body. You'll build up discipline and determination. You'll become more structured and persistent. You will actually start to become a new and improved version of yourself, one who possesses strength that the former self did not have. So, what I'm really talking about here is a process of transformation. What you have done thus far is a reflection of who it is that you have become up to this point, and what you achieve in the future will be a product of who you have become between now and then.

At every moment in life, you have a choice. You can sit back and watch life pass you by, or you can get out and do something worthwhile. You can settle for an unfulfilled life, or take the reins of your own destiny. If you are ready to take action and do those things that will fill your life with purpose, now is the time to get committed. You need to assume an attitude of being relentless. Anyone can go out and put in a halfhearted effort toward achieving his or her goals, but doing that won't get you the kind of results you want. The people who get what they desire in life are those who are willing to give it a hundred percent every time. Of course, you'll have days when your energy level is low or you just don't get up to your normal speed. The key lies in making these days the exception and not the rule.

Part of your process should be about making improvements. Make it a habit to reserve a part of your day for self-reflection. You must know exactly where you are in pursuit of your goals at any moment, because looking back on your activities and accomplishments, in this way, will give you valuable and real-time feedback. Think about where you could have increased your efforts. Is there an area of your life where you could possibly be more consistent? Think about what it is that you can do better tomorrow.

You've already created your life's master plan. Now it is time to work it like nobody else can, and remember to fine-tune that plan as you go along. This is a long-distance run, not a sprint. There will be times when adjustments are necessary. Make them and move on. Just remember to always adjust things in the direction of progress.

Each goal is like a target, something that you can set your sights on and shoot for, and it can be very exhilarating to reach such a desired outcome. However, the real value of going after what you want lies in who you find yourself becoming in the process, while enjoying the process itself.

There are many reasons why it's of paramount importance to enjoy the process. First of all, your original goal may change any number of times as you pursue it. If your only focus is on getting to the end result, each of these adjustments may feel like a miniature failure. When you appreciate the journey, however, you know that every turn is simply another leg of the trip. Second, your goal may be something that is too enormous to achieve all at once. You might need to go after a smaller achievement that sets you up to knock down the big one. It's good to have high expectations, but becoming attached to those that are too lofty can prepare you for an intimate relationship with heartbreak and despair. Paying attention to the process will help you remain emotionally centered as you come into contact with unexpected roadblocks.

You can derive a great feeling of satisfaction from knowing that you are moving toward a higher quality of life. Often, this feeling is more important than that precise goal that you seek to achieve. It allows you to feel good about each day, instead of making your joy contingent on some future event. It's also easier to learn about life when you're taking time to enjoy your day-to-day activities and accomplishments. A process-centered focus actually keeps you engaged with what's happening in each moment. This makes learning occur almost automatically. Often, people don't make appropriate adjustments because they're mentally stuck in either the past or future. This can't happen, though, when you're paying attention to changes that occur in real time. The goal is merely an end result. Sure, getting to it will feel great for a while, but eventually, that feeling of triumph is likely to fade. On the other hand, that experience of growing and evolving is something that remains with you for life. So it's important to pay attention to what's happening as you go along. That's where you will find the real substance of experience.

CHAPTER IV:

WORKSHEET

List three notable people that you admire or who have achieved what you would like to achieve.

Study the biographies or autobiographies of these people. What are some of the things they routinely did that had a positive impact on their successes?

How did your models describe the way they conceptualized challenges and obstacles?

What were their views on perseverance and determination?

In what ways would you need to think differently in order to implement some of these strategies in your own life?

What parts of your current daily routine do you need to change or eliminate?

How do you need to use your time differently to get more of what you want out of life?

List one time in your life when you went for a goal and considered no other option but success.

What did you do, mentally, that allowed you to persevere and achieve that goal?

What would happen if you did that same thing with the goals you seek to achieve now?

PART I: PREPARATION

CHAPTER V

Getting Into the Right State

Think of what you want out of life. If you look behind those desires, you'll find that what you *really* want is some type of feeling that you believe achieving this goal will bring you. Think about it for a second. What we all really want out of life are positive emotions. We want to feel good, and everything we do is either geared toward bringing on more of the feelings we do want into our lives or less of those we don't want.

Let's consider a typical goal of many people: making more money. Does a person really just want to accumulate money, piles of paper with no inherent value? Or does he or she want the things he or she thinks that money will bring, such as a better lifestyle and the ability to travel and have amazing experiences? Let's take this idea even further. Why would a person desire those types of things? If you continue exploring, you'll see that people eventually want the things that they think will make them feel better. People who want more money do so because they believe that having it will give them the ability to do or have certain things. They further believe that those things would give them an increased sense of freedom, security, confidence, fun or any number of other positive emotions. Emotions are what move us. We do what we do because we think that it will help us to feel a certain way. Understanding this is a huge step forward on the path of personal achievement. If you want to improve your behavior, then you need to improve the way you feel on a typical basis. You have to work on getting into the right emotional state—the right state of mind.

When you're in the right state of mind, everything you want to do happens naturally and effortlessly. Have you ever been in a situation when you were speaking about something that you were really passionate about and all the right words just seemed to flow out of your mouth? In that particular state, you could do no wrong. Your responses were sharp and intelligent. You had an appropriate answer for every question that came your way. This is because how you perform depends on the emotional state you're in at the time. You've probably had other experiences in which you knew the subject matter thoroughly, but just couldn't seem to say anything right. That happened because you were in a less resourceful state of mind at the time.

You know that when you feel good, you think more clearly and perform much better. Conversely, when you feel bad, it's hard to make anything go right. You can, in fact, do much more than you ever imagined. However, you will often do much less than you are capable of, unless you learn how to put yourself in an empowering state. The fact is that when you're in a fantastic state of mind, you'll get much more out of yourself than when you aren't. What you want to do, then, is go after those empowering feelings and attach them to achieving your goal.

Things that are happening outside of you don't determine how you feel. Let's say that you wanted to go outside and have a picnic, but then you suddenly discovered that it was raining. You might start to feel a little "down in the dumps." Now, say you were a farmer in the same town who had not seen rain fall on his crops in weeks. You would have a much different experience, wouldn't you? You'd probably feel overjoyed, thinking about how your harvest would flourish now that your crops had water. In each situation, you would be choosing what to feel, based on your personal desires and thoughts of the moment. Often, we are unaware of this process because it seems like things just happen to make us feel a certain way. However, nothing actually makes you feel anything. It is only the meaning that you give to an event that decides what emotional state you will experience because of it.

Your state largely depends on what you are focusing upon at any given moment. Thinking of the things that are going wrong in your life leads you to feel frustrated, tense and at a loss for hope. However, when you think about what you have to be grateful for, you end up feeling hopeful, confident and empowered to do more. So what we want to do is make sure that we are in the right emotional state to pursue our goals with utmost confidence, determination and clarity.

One way you can learn to feel more empowered is to examine what you already do to get in that state. We've all had those "in the zone" moments, times when it seemed like everything you did worked out just right. You need to notice what you were doing at that time, in both your body and mind, and practice performing that same process when it matters most. Think about the way that you move when you're in an ideal state. How do you breathe, gesture, form facial expressions and talk? How do you stand and walk when you feel totally confident and empowered? Think about these things carefully and write your findings down. Noticing how you behave in an ideal state will let you know how to perform your best in the future. When you feel confident, you probably stand, gesture and speak in a certain way. You also stand, gesture, and speak in a certain way when you're feeling down or depressed. So one of the things you can do to improve your state is to practice holding a "posture of power." This means making the quality of your behavior the same as it is when you feel confident. You want to stand, breathe, gesture and move as you do when you're in an empowered state. You want to speak in the same tone and tempo as you do when you feel your best. Acting in this way gives signals to your brain that it's time to feel totally confident and empowered.

Another thing you can do to achieve a wonderful emotional state is consciously pay attention to things that make you feel good. When you're constantly thinking about negative things, like debt and lack, it's really hard to get into a positive state. However, when you focus on opportunities, blessings or the promise that life has to offer, you automatically start to feel better. I'm not saying that you should ignore obstacles and challenges that come your way, but it's much more empowering to think of solutions instead of problems.

We can only pay attention to a small amount of information at any given time. You always have an opportunity to experience the state you want, but if you get in the habit of focusing on the negative, that's all you'll see. It will seem like your entire world is wrapped in problems. I know this might sound like a storm of positive thinking advocacy, but I assure you, I'm the kind of person who appreciates tangible results, not just positive words and thoughts stranded in midair. I bet you come from the same school of thought, or you wouldn't be reading this book! Let me give you a quick and practical example of how our focus can control what we feel in a way that goes far beyond mere "positive thinking."

Have you ever gotten a cut on your arm or hand sometime during the day, but were so occupied with what you were doing that you didn't even notice it? Later, when you jumped into the shower or washed your hands, that cut probably started to sting. At a time like that, it's very natural to look down in surprise and think, "Wow, when did I get that?" While you were fully engaged in your daily tasks, you didn't have the extra attention to notice that the cut was there. Your brain was actually deleting the pain sensation from your awareness, so that you could focus on more pressing matters. That's the problem with thinking about what you don't want on a consistent basis. Your brain will actually start ignoring any occasions to feel good. This is why a bad day typically gets worse and a good day is likely to get even better. Your brain is always looking for opportunities to draw more of what you focus on into your awareness.

How you talk to yourself also has a big impact on what you pay attention to. If you tell yourself things like, "I never have enough money," "Things just don't work out for me," or "I'll never get ahead," your brain will accept those statements as instructions. It will then do whatever it needs to make sure that you get exactly what you expect. On the other hand, if you say, "Things will work out in the end" or "Opportunity is just around the corner," your brain will make sure that you notice things that cause those words to be true. You see, your brain has been elegantly designed and programmed to obey your very commands. Consequently, it will obey your orders at any time. Orders accepted by the brain are often given meaning through words. To put it another way, how you talk to yourself will dictate the exact orders your brain will worshipfully follow.

We all have the power to control our emotional states. However, most people don't utilize this ability at all. Many just go aimlessly through the day, letting people, circumstances and events decide how they will feel. When something good happens, they feel good. When something happens that they don't want, they feel bad. The person who lives like this has no control over his or her own emotions. His or her life becomes nothing but a series of reactions, and the most he or she can do is hope that a positive sequence of events will "magically" fall into place. If you want to create the life of your dreams, however, you need to consciously choose your thoughts and actions. You must get in the habit of directing your mind and body in a way that serves your ambitions. A person who has not developed the ability to focus is like a moving vehicle with no driver. Any bump in the road sends him or her swerving off in another direction. He or she is one of those habitual starters—a person who's full of new ideas, but has no follow-through whatsoever. It's no wonder that this type of person typically remains in the same conditions, year after year.

Keep in mind that there is lots of information coming at you, from numerous directions, virtually all of the time. Your ability to filter out distractions and concentrate on one thing will largely determine your rate of progress. So, whatever the first step is for you on the road to achievement, you've got to work on that task with everything you've got. Too many distractions will simply slow you down and make your road to success much longer than it needs to be. Once you've mastered one thing, move on. It's very easy to get sidetracked by "the next big thing," but successful people aren't focused on doing what's easy. They make the effort to do what needs to be done at any particular moment. Don't worry that you'll miss out on something great if you don't give your attention to everything that comes along. It will all be worthwhile when you see yourself systematically making progress. Learn this skill and you will become better at doing virtually everything you attempt. It will also keep you from being overwhelmed by thinking about too many things at once. Anxiety can easily take root in an unfocused mind.

However, being focused is not the same as being irrationally stubborn. You must be single-minded about your purpose, yet flexible in the way that you choose to achieve your goals. Concentrate fully on what you're doing in any moment, but alter your approach when necessary. Concentrate on your ambitions, but keep your eyes open to cues that tell you when a change in strategy is required.

CHAPTER V:

WORKSHEET

Power Posture

Just recall a time in your life when you felt powerful and confident. In your mind, go back to that moment, as though you were there right now. Become aware of what you see, hear and feel. Notice what you're doing and what you're thinking about, as you feel that sense of total confidence. Stand up for a moment to make this experience as real as possible. Take all the time you need to go deeper into that experience and into that sense of power and confidence.

As you fully relive that experience now, answer the following questions:

How do you stand when you feel powerful and confident?

How do you move and gesture?

How do you breathe when you feel this way?

Are your shoulders slumped forward or pulled back?
In what position are you holding your head?

When you feel like this, what are the tempo and tone of your voice like?

The above list is a detailed description of what your "Posture of Power" looks like. Repeat these behaviors when you need to quickly boost your mood.

Controlling Your Focus

What are you grateful for? No matter who you are, everyone has something to be thankful for. For instance, if you're reading this book, then you have eyes to see with, know how to read, and have the mental presence to improve your life. Take some time to list everything you can think of to be appreciative for in your life.

When you are feeling bad, what type of things would you typically be thinking of?

What are some of the more positive aspects of the same situations that you could focus on instead?

What lessons have you learned from facing challenges in the past?

What could be the long-term value of some of the challenges you're facing today?

Have you ever looked back at some of the problems you experienced in the past and realized that things weren't as bad as they seemed then?

Do you see that in a future time you may look back at today and discover the same thing?

If you will be able to understand that in the future, wouldn't it be easier to just think that way now?

What steps will you take this week to focus more on what you have to be grateful for, instead of on problems?

CHAPTER V:

Bonus Exercise: Anchoring for Success

This next exercise will guide you through a process commonly known as "Anchoring." It works according to the "conditioned reflex" principle, discovered by renowned Russian physiologist Ivan Pavlov.

Pavlov discovered that he could use a sound to stimulate an unconscious response in animals. He rang a particular bell each time he fed a group of hungry dogs in his lab. Naturally, the dogs would salivate when they realized that food was on the way. After doing this several times, Pavlov found that he could make the dogs salivate merely by ringing the bell, even in the absence of food. The dogs had been conditioned to respond to a stimulus, the bell, through salivation. Now, salivation is an unconscious process, which means that the dogs didn't consciously force themselves to salivate. It was a process that happened all by itself, whereby the dogs' bodies, if you will, thought that they were receiving nourishment, and responded accordingly by salivating. Does that make sense?

Let me approach this from another angle. In mathematics, we all know that if "X" equals "Y", then "Y" equals "X," right? For better understanding, let's define the following:

X = the dogs are eating

Y = the bell is ringing

So every single time X was happening, Y was happening simultaneously. In other words, every single time the dogs were eating, the bell was ringing. After pairing this many many times, Pavlov made one of his most intriguing discoveries. He was able to condition the dogs in such a way that when he rang the bell, the dogs' bodies "thought" that they were eating, and hence salivated! So when Y happened, the dogs' unconscious bodies thought that X was happening, although in reality it wasn't.

Soon after, it was discovered that the conditioned response principle also applies to human beings. If a person can get into a highly emotional state and pair it with a unique stimulus over and over again, that stimulus will be able to unconsciously trigger the emotional response at will! So, whenever you feel a powerful emotion and simultaneously experience a sensory stimulus, like a touch or sound, your brain associates the two. It then causes one event to automatically trigger the other. Hearing a particular song can take you back to a wonderful childhood memory. A certain smell may cause you to feel just as you did during a holiday celebration years ago. Those triggers are commonly known as "anchors" in the world of peak performance.

Next, we're going to install some anchors to be fired at will. In order for this process to work, I advise you to read the following text several times until you master the overall idea. Once you're ready, sit back, close your eyes, and begin the first step toward self mastery, installing your anchors for success.

Find a place where you can sit back or lay back comfortably. When you are comfortable, just recall a specific time in your life when you felt completely unstoppable. You can think of something that happened yesterday, last week, last month, last year, or any time in your past. Just go back to a moment when you felt totally confident, like you could accomplish anything you set your mind to. As you remember that time in your life when you felt unstoppable, I'd like you to bring back everything you can about that experience. Think of who else may or may not have been there. Remember everything you saw, what you could hear, and any feelings that you sense coming into your awareness. Allow yourself to become fully absorbed in that moment. Go all the way into that experience, so that you even remember how you breathed when you felt totally confident and unstoppable. Notice where you can sense those feelings inside of your body right now, and as you focus on those feelings, just allow them to increase and expand, so that they begin to spread out and grow stronger. Notice how that feeling of being unstoppable gets stronger and stronger just by focusing on it. Let it spin all throughout your body, over and over again, and allow it to spread out and intensify until it starts to spin some more and you find it moving through every cell of your body.

Now, think about how your breathing would change if that feeling were to become twice as powerful right now. As you feel that, notice how the feeling moves and spins even faster. When that feeling becomes really powerful and intense, and only then, press the thumb and middle finger of one hand together. Hold that pressure between the two fingers. When you feel the feeling starting to fade, release the fingers and relax. Do this process at least fifteen times to install a proper anchor. Remember, you must press your fingers together at the peak of the emotional experience. Anything less than the peak would render this whole process useless. Later, when you wish to reignite that sense of being totally confident and unstoppable, press those two fingers together. This will act as a triggering mechanism that releases those powerful feelings back into your body and mind.

What we did in this exercise is anchor the feeling of being unstoppable to the stimulus of pressing two fingers together. The more you activate this trigger, the easier it will become to do so. Each time, you'll be strengthening the neural pathways that your brain has created to associate the action and emotion.

Athletes do this sort of thing all the time. An elite performer will usually have a pregame ritual that he or she uses to get into a highly focused state of mind. A baseball player may twirl the bat and shuffle his feet in a particular way every single time he steps up to the plate. A football player may smack his helmet six times on each side before taking the field. These customs are actually anchors that resurrect desired mental and emotional states. Now you know why peak performers do what they do without their actually knowing of how the process works. They often link it to good luck, or being in "the zone."

After you're done installing your anchor, keep your eyes closed and think of how you could use this principle in your daily life. Imagine going into an important meeting or event and firing off that ultimate confidence trigger. Consider what it would be like to step into a high pressure situation and instantly bring forth that sense of feeling absolutely unstoppable. How would you perform differently, knowing that you could truly achieve whatever you desired?

Just like a professional athlete, you too can call upon your most valuable internal resources when it matters most. Practice activating this confidence trigger whenever it is useful in your daily life.

Getting Into the Right Spot

Okay, so you've learned how to get into the right state for success. Now it's time to get into the right spot. What do I mean by this? I mean that you have to put yourself in a place where the opportunity to get what you want is likely to emerge. Think about this. No matter how many goals you set, no matter how many books you read about achieving success, what you want is not likely to come knocking down your door. You need to put yourself in position to make things happen.

If you want to be a famous actor, you need to be at auditions. You must go places where you'll have the opportunity to act. If you want to get in better shape, you need to be at the gym, on the track, in the pool or in front of the workout machine in your home. If you want to be a chef, you need to attend some cooking classes or be in a restaurant interviewing for the position. You will not get in shape in the comfort of your living room couch. You will not make sales unless you are on the phone or in front of a prospect. With whatever you want, there's some place where your probability of getting it goes up, and what you must do is get in the habit of being wherever that is.

We all know that the hardest step toward making change is the first one. Once you're in position, however, you are more likely to get started. It's easy to skip a day of exercise if you stay in bed and hit the snooze button. However, if you get into your clothes and go to the gym, you're likely to go ahead and get a workout. If you go into the yard with your gardening gloves on, it's very likely that you will pull a few weeds. This principle works so well because it gets you out of the "tomorrow" syndrome, where you substitute taking action now for a promise to do so "tomorrow." We all know that tomorrow usually turns into next week, next month and next year, but our brains are wonderful tricksters that keep us believing that tomorrow will actually come.

Sometimes we can get so overwhelmed by the magnitude of what lies ahead that a part of us associates the very act of getting started with pain, but if you just get into that first position, the place where the first step needs to happen, you'll probably notice that it doesn't seem so difficult after all. Once you've completed that, the next thing to do won't be so far out of reach.

Until you put yourself in that first position, what you want is just a wish. You don't have any potential to make things happen until you put yourself in the right place. It's important to dream and envision your goals, but never forget the value of setting yourself up for success. A big part of being great is just showing up. I once read of a lady who'd won hundreds of magazine contests and sweepstakes. When asked to reveal her secret, she said that ninety percent of people who enter such competitions don't follow the rules accurately. These people are quickly eliminated by the ruling board without ever even having a chance to win. The contest-winning woman put herself in position, and just by following the entry instructions, she consistently moved ahead of almost everyone else. What small thing could you do right now, tomorrow, this week that would move you ahead? In what ways can you "show up" and put yourself in a better position to achieve your goals?

"Luck is when opportunity meets preparation," it's often said. What an interesting and true concept! Luck is nothing more than opportunity stopping by and saying, "Are you ready for this? Are you ready to take advantage of what I have to offer?" When you think of things this way, it emphasizes the importance of preparing yourself for success. When you are prepared, when you're ready to take the ball into your hands and run with it, others may believe that some sort of supernatural force is working in your favor. But you will know the truth—you have created your own "good luck." If you are not prepared to seize opportunity when one comes up, however, you won't become "lucky." In fact, you may not even realize that something good has just passed through your fingers. This type of preparation might be about studying and organizing your ideas. It might involve practicing and rehearsing for your desired role. You can't rely on getting your act together at the last minute. Chances are that it will be too late to make a difference.

Life is made up of moments. In actuality, each moment holds within it an opportunity to learn, to experience, to try new things, and to become your very best. Time and energy are our two most valuable resources. Both are limited—none of us really know how much we have and you can't get either one back once it's gone. Therefore, how you decide to use your time and energy, day-in and day-out, is of the utmost importance.

The habits that hurt you most are probably those that waste your time and energy. The key lies in figuring out what to pay attention to and what to ignore. There are all sorts of things that can take your mind off what matters most. This is why we must make a point to continually prioritize our daily tasks. You may have a habitual urge to participate in certain activities, but many of these tasks may add little or no real value to your true life's purpose. When you involve yourself in something, it should be for a reason. This is the difference between living intentionally and simply reacting to whatever comes your way.

CHAPTER VI:

WORKSHEET

What are the things that you most want to achieve?

For each goal listed above, how could you position yourself differently to increase your chances of success?

Name at least one thing that you will do today to place yourself in line for success.

What are some of the initial preparation steps that you can take for each goal listed earlier?

What are some things you can start doing now that others in your field are not doing?

CHAPTER VII

Getting Ready to Make It Happen

Getting ready to make it happen is the hidden key of preparation. This step involves anticipating typical challenges that are likely to come your way. I once studied the biography of a lawyer who had won over ninety-five percent of his cases. He said that building your case carefully for trial is essential to success, but he also pointed out something that many people overlook when pursuing a goal. He said that it's also of utmost importance to study your opponent's perspective. That way, you can pre-arrange an appropriate response for almost anything that comes up in court.

When you choose to go after your dreams, you will encounter many obstacles along the way, but you don't have to be sidelined by every awkward occurrence that pops up. If you put a little pre-thought into your efforts, you'll discover that many challenges can be foreseen and dealt with before they ever have a chance of taking root.

Let's use the example of a person who wants to improve her public speaking skills. She has plans to deliver a beautiful presentation, has accumulated all of the necessary facts and has organized them logically. However, let's examine what might happen if she were to concentrate on performing this essential step. She may find out that a certain fraction of her audience is opposed to the presented topic. She could take initiative in learning what the common arguments are and compile evidence that shows why her position in valid. When the day comes for her to speak, she will be ready to take on challenges from peers.

If you apply the same principle to your own efforts, it will seem as though you have the magic touch. Others will be amazed to discover how well organized your thoughts and actions are. You could have a beautifully orchestrated plan and put yourself in all the right places, but if your strategy is not built to withstand attack, your work will fall flat before very long. As you travel the road to your dreams, there will be naysayers; there will be critics; there will be those who try to sabotage your success, either consciously or unconsciously. That is why you have to fortify yourself for battle.

Achieving success is definitely not a task for wimps. If you really want more out of life and you're serious about getting it, you have to be ready to fight the good fight. You have to be relentless, someone who confronts necessary challenges instead of ducking them.

Now I want you to think of some area of your life that you'd like to improve. When you have that goal firmly in mind, ask yourself, "If I attempt to achieve this, what's the worst that can happen?" Really try to think of the worst possible thing that could happen if you try to achieve your goal. If you've really taken time to consider the worst possible outcome, you'll probably notice at least one of two things. Firstly, the worst-case-scenario that you came up with might not be as bad as you once thought it would be. Secondly, you know that what you fear is likely to never happen. That's right, most of the horrors that we project into the future never even happen. Our minds often play cruel tricks on us, and they're really, really good at it. However, there's an even better reason for performing this thought exercise. Now you can prepare for the worst possible outcome of pursuing your goals. You can design a strategy to minimize any negative effects that would occur if your worst fear were to come to fruition. In fact, make two or three contingency plans, in case the first one doesn't pan out. When you have thoroughly prepared for the absolute worst, what is left to fear?

In order to fully express this concept, I'm going to take a page from the world of boxing. Insiders know that boxing is the art of "hitting without getting hit." The interesting thing is that the last part of that phrase is more important than the first. See, a prizefighter with even moderate skill is likely to score a few punches on his adversary during any fight. The trick lies in keeping his opponent from landing anything solid. A fighter who can master the art of defense is likely to win many battles.

As you move toward your goals, life is going to throw heavy punches at you, from every angle imaginable. Your environment will try to hold you back. Your surroundings have been created in a way that supports the lifestyle you have right now, and when you attempt to break out of your present conditions, it may seem as though everything around you is just trying to get in the way of your progress. People may say things like, "Why are you spending so much time on that?" or "It doesn't seem like what you're doing has helped you much so far." You may be in an area where people don't put much effort into doing better. The same unfocused friends that you hung out with before are likely to stop by and do their best to knock you off course. This is not to say that the people who you are familiar with have anything against you. They probably like you a lot. They are just doing what they have previously programmed themselves to do. They are living their own reality—a reality filled with limitations and fears. You were once a part of that world, so it's very natural for those people to try and get you back on board. However, you have made a deliberate choice to improve the quality of your life. This choice, like all others, comes at a price. Your new reality can only emerge as the old one falls away. In order to make this happen successfully, you must adequately prepare yourself for the conflict ahead. You can't plan for everything, of course, but you can take steps to dramatically increase your chances of success.

One way you can reinforce and strengthen your resolve to succeed is to get a hold of your big "WHY." Your "WHY" is your primary driver; it is what most moves you toward your principal goal. Why do you want more money? Is it because you want to do more for your family, have more time with the kids, or create more adventure or excitement in your life? Why do you want to become an excellent communicator? Do you want to empower others or have a positive impact on society? The end result of your goal stands as the big "WHY" for fulfilling your dreams. This is the reason that you will hold on to whenever challenges come your way. Your big "WHY" is the fuel that will propel you past obstacles, setbacks and difficulties.

Below is a questionnaire and exercise form that you can use to discover your "WHY" and use it to drive you toward success.

CHAPTER VII:

WORKSHEET

Below, make a list of what motivates you to improve in different areas of your life.

Family

Financial

Career

Education

Personal Development

Other

For each of the aforementioned categories, write down what having that list of things would give you.
Family

Financial

Career

Education

Personal Development

Other

What would having those things allow you to give?
Family

Financial

Career

Education

Personal Development

Other

What would that help you to become more of?

What impact would these things enable you to make on your family, friends, society and the world at large?

How will that allow you to feel?

Why will you do whatever it takes to achieve those goals?

The last few questions will help you get in touch with your "WHY." Your big "WHY" will keep you going when times get tough. Go back to this list often, perhaps every day, to keep in touch with your reasons for pursuing your goals.

PART III: TAKING ACTION

CHAPTER VIII

The Two Big E's

Before we kick this off, I would like to salute you for committing to continue this journey with me thus far. Your persistence and your eagerness to improve the quality of your life fill my heart with warmth and joy.

Next, I'm going to introduce you to a concept I came up with several years ago, one I like to call "The Two Big E's." As you probably noticed, I'm a great fan, student and teacher of human performance. One thing that has always fascinated me is the brain's ability to develop and run certain programs. What captivates me even more is the fact that once our brains accept a certain program, they adopt the program as true and reinforce it into our values and beliefs. The two E's that I speak of are Emotion and Experience. Both of these elements must be present before a person's brain will adopt any new program. The combination of emotion and experience underlies every habitual pattern, be it good or bad. In this section, however, we're going to explore how that combination works to create and maintain common problems.

Let's start with the first "E," Emotion. Remember, emotions are what move and drive us. Our actions and desires are guided by what we believe will give us positive emotional experiences. In order to make this concept clear, we'll use the example of a young woman who has been dealing with weight-control issues for most of her life.

This person's problem with food started early. One day, she returned home from school feeling very down and depressed. Her mother, sensing a dilemma, said, "Why don't you have a scoop of ice cream? It'll make you feel better." The girl liked ice cream and she did want to feel better, so she quickly agreed. The important thing to remember is that this little girl primarily wanted the emotions that she thought having ice cream would give her. Now, we move on to the second "E," Experience. As the young girl ate the ice cream, she instantly became absorbed in its delicious flavor. This served to distract her mind from the problems at hand. The sugar gave her a quick boost of energy and a brief emotional "pick-me-up." When food entered her stomach, certain biochemicals were released that actually made her feel better for a short time. So the girl initially wanted the first "E," the emotion, and she then had the "Experience" of getting what she was after. The next time this little girl started to feel bad, she reached for a bowl of ice cream. The quick payoff she received encouraged her to manage other emotions with food. She started to eat when she felt bored, lonely, frustrated or angry. Simultaneously, she neglected developing the ability to resolve such issues on her own. In the end, she became dependent on food for feelings, and she became locked inside a problem from which she did not know how to escape.

The emotion and experience equation applies to all negative patterns of behavior. A person does something in order to feel a certain way. That action creates an often short-term experience of getting the desired result. The experience then drives the person to continue seeking the emotion in this way. The cycle goes on, until it becomes a habitual pattern that persists without thought. Often, we create these associations outside of conscious awareness. The person using food for comfort has no idea why she can't simply stop eating things that are bad for her. Just like Pavlov's conditioned reflex phenomena, her brain has "wired" food and comfort together. This is true, whether the addiction is to smoking, drugs, gambling, shopping or anything else.

I've coached more people than I can count to break out of their programs and develop a healthier lifestyle. All these people, no matter what their background, shared a common denominator— subconscious programming. Believe it or not, our brains just don't seem to care about our socioeconomic status or intellectual level. Once the brain perceives a potential program, it goes on to testing it. If the program passes the test, it is then adopted as a "bulletproof" strategy. That's why it becomes so hard to consciously convince ourselves to give up a certain habit. After all, the conscious mind cannot "deprogram" a subconscious strategy!

The good news is that now that you know about this programming, it becomes easy for you to give up old unwanted habits. If you can figure out the emotion your brain is trying to satisfy and find a healthier way to satisfy that same emotion, your brain will probably adopt this new program as a strategy. With enough practice, you will be able to completely dissolve the old program and make way for the new one.

As you proceed to doing the next worksheet, I invite you to be brutally honest with yourself. The more time, thought, and honesty you apply to doing this exercise, the more beneficial it will become. Enjoy your worksheet, and I'll be eagerly waiting to continue serving you on the following pages.

CHAPTER VIII:

WORKSHEET

List a particular habitual behavior pattern that you'd like to change.

When did you first start this behavior?

At that time, what did you believe taking this action would do for you?

When the habit began, what made it seem like this behavior was giving you what you wanted?

How did the combination of Emotion and Experience work together in creating this habit?

How do they encourage behavioral patterns to continue?

What have you learned from seeing this connection?

What is the specific emotion you are trying to satisfy by engaging in this habit?

List some healthier ways to satisfy that same emotion.

What kind of experience will you be expecting after adopting this healthier habit?

How many experiences do you need to verify this new program?

What resources do you already have that will help you obtain your outcome?

What resources do you still need?

What's the first step you plan on taking now to get you closer to your outcome?

CHAPTER IX

Designing a Foolproof Mentality

Now we're going to talk about how to approach your goals in a way that ensures success. Yes, it's true that there are no guarantees in life, and you can never be sure that anything will work out in the way you expect. However, you can develop an outlook that guarantees your personal success no matter what obstacles come your way. This is what I call designing a foolproof mentality.

You may have heard the phrase "Every cloud has a silver lining." Every result you produce contains a benefit. Every outcome has value. The key lies in figuring out how whatever you encounter can work to your advantage. Once you understand this concept, every movement you make is a step forward. Perception makes a huge impact on performance. The only meaning of any event that occurs in your life is the one you assign it. Just as there are at least two sides to every story, there are numerous ways you can look at anything that happens.

People in our society are addicted to outcomes. We're brought up believing that things simply not turning out as we've planned is the same as failure. I couldn't disagree more. Every situation you encounter on the way to attaining your goals can be used to your advantage. Let's take the following scenario as an example.

You were just hired by a well-known manufacturing firm. Your job description requires you to make one hundred sales calls per day. Now, you want to be a fantastic salesperson—that's your goal. You know what you want, are quite driven and, like all of us, have an ability to learn. However, suppose you don't make an intentional effort to create the mindset of success. You are simply relying on enthusiasm to move you forward. So, the workweek begins and you start making calls. The first person you talk to is extremely rude and discourteous. He hangs up on you without a moment's hesitation, and you feel a little let down from the experience. The second call goes pretty much the same way. Again, you feel disappointed about what has occurred. Time and time again, throughout the day, you come in contact with people who have no interest in what you offer. A few people stay on the line long enough to hear you out. However, they all close the door on your idea at some point. At the close of business you feel incredibly frustrated, beaten up and discouraged.

Now, let's see what would have happened had you taken the time to develop a foolproof mentality. The night before your first day of work, you are at home mentally preparing yourself for the job. You might say things to yourself like, "I know that I have the capability to be a great salesperson. Selling is a skill and I can learn anything I set mind to. It may be rough at first, but if I keep going and continue to find new ways of approaching prospects, I'm sure to hit my mark. If I make a sale, that's great! Even if I get turned down, it will let me know how I can get better. I'll keep saying things that work well for me. If a part of my presentation falls flat, I'll cut it out of the script or find a new way of wording it. I don't care which result I get right now, because either will help me become fantastic at making sales."

Can you see the difference? If you adopt the second attitude, you cannot lose. When you see a benefit in both outcomes and are equally prepared to accept either one, you have truly developed a foolproof mindset. You don't have to worry about any one event holding you back, as you view every circumstance in a way that moves you forward.

Your outlook will determine the resources, opportunities and choices that you perceive to be available to you in any given situation. If you keep the big picture in focus, you won't be sidelined by the setbacks of a single day. This gives you the incredible power to choose your outcomes instead of falling prey to them.

The "Foolproof Mentality" principle is about setting yourself up to win. If you can choose your mental experiences, why not select those that empower you, those that make you stronger? Reality is not as fixed as we often think. What you focus on becomes real to you. If you concentrate on setbacks, obstacles and things that you can't do, that is all you'll ever end up with. However, if you choose to view every event as an opportunity to learn and grow, you'll find the lessons you seek.

You can only fail by accepting defeat. However, if you look at your results and say, "How can I make this better?" you're still on the path to success. The problem is that most people neglect to assume authority over their own reality. If you don't control your thoughts, they will run rampant and probably produce results that you don't want. Without direction, your brain will be more likely to latch onto any fear, doubt or worry that pops up. It may seem like these things are real, but they are merely the outpourings of an undisciplined mind. If you don't intentionally select a resourceful state of mind, you will end up merely reacting to circumstances instead of responding appropriately.

When you take care to design a foolproof mentality, every day is productive. As you focus on the positive aspects of every situation, your RAS (Reticular Activating System) will seek out opportunities to do even better. You'll start to see the world in a whole new way, one that makes you capable of achieving much more than you ever imagined. This is the power of choice in action, and it is your right to use this ability to your advantage in every situation.

Some of us fall into the trap of getting too much information before making the first move. You may decide that you want to become really good at something and set off to learn everything you can about the subject. Of course, it's good to be well-educated about whatever you choose to participate in. However, in order to create the kind of results you want, you also have to be willing to take massive action.

As an example, think about a young boy who wants to be a really great soccer player. The first thing he does is check out every book in the library about soccer. He studies and studies and studies, learning every technique there is about soccer and even little-known secrets of the game. After maybe a month or so, he decides to try out his skill set on the field. Soon, he gets to participate in a soccer game, ready to show everyone what he's learned. Before long, however, it becomes apparent that the boy does not play soccer very well. He finds it very difficult to do the things he has read about and looks like a complete novice on the field. The important thing, however, is what this boy tells himself after the game. He decides that his failure to perform indicates that he just hasn't learned enough. He decides to resolve this problem by reading more books. So he reads and reads and reads again. The next time he goes out to play, he performs just as badly. Disappointed and frustrated, he chooses to give up the sport, figuring that he just doesn't have what it takes to be great at soccer.

When you look at this scenario from a logical approach, you realize the boy made some crucial errors along the way. He believed that learning, by itself, was power. In truth, however, learning is only *potential* power. Action is actually the element that moves you forward. It is only "doing" that has the ability to make you great at anything.

Even though the boy absorbed an incredible amount of information, it is no surprise that he couldn't perform on the field. Knowing has no influence over your life by itself. Our boy had all of the best moves in his head, but he lacked the ability to execute them. He needed to strengthen certain tendons, muscles and bones. He had to practice doing challenging maneuvers over and over again until they became ingrained in his neurology. This is the only way that he could have become good at playing soccer.

The same things are true for you. You can't become great at phone sales without making calls. You can't become a great communicator without talking to people. You could spend your entire life studying, yet never develop the tools that you need to succeed. You can read everything there is to know about swimming, but until you get into the water and can carry out what you've learned, you won't really know how to swim. There are numerous aspects of any experience that outside information simply will not explain to you. There can be a big difference between knowing something in theory and making it work, and in order to make it work, you must have a foolproof mentality that will set you up for absolute success.

CHAPTER IX:

WORKSHEET

In what parts of your life could you use more mental resilience?

What would it mean for you to achieve massive success in these areas?

What challenges are you likely to face when attempting to improve in these parts of your life?

What are some ways you could benefit from the abovementioned difficulties? For example, losing money on an investment may end up giving you business experience that will make you highly successful in the future.

How could you look at things so that both victory and defeat give you an advantage in these areas?

What kind of things could you say to yourself that would make you willing to accept either result?

How does it feel to know that you "win," no matter what the outcome?

What would you attempt to do, if you knew that it was impossible to fail?

CHAPTER X

Do Something!

Nothing takes place without action. Nothing will change in your life until you do something different. Direction is in the design. However, it is only action that creates progress. Everything you have right now in your life is the result of the things you do on a consistent basis. I repeat this point often because I want it to stick. If you want something different out of life, then your behavior has to change in some way. If you always find yourself showing up late to gatherings, meetings or appointments, then just planning to be on time is not going to cut it. Perhaps you should practice leaving the door thirty minutes earlier to account for unexpected delays in traffic. You may want to adjust the speed of your morning ritual by moving faster or cutting out wasteful activities that take up your time.

If you want to have more influence at your place of work, you can work at gaining others' trust by becoming a great listener. You could express your ideas more assertively and make sure that you stand up to speak during meetings. You might want to go to your boss and ask if you can take on new and more challenging projects.

If you want to have better relationships, you can spend more time talking about the other person's interests, or maybe you need to put more of your own preferences into play, so that your partner will have a deeper appreciation for you as an individual. You may want to set aside time each week for sharing goals and dreams or for just having fun.

There are numerous ways to improve any area of your life. The key, however, is to do something different. Many people set a goal and then just continue following the same old daily routine—or even worse, they do more of what they've done in the past and magnify the circumstances they don't want. One of the reasons this happens is that most people strongly resist changing what they're accustomed to. The human mind is drawn to the familiar. It seeks to create more of what it already knows. This is true even when what we know doesn't work. You see this happening all around you. The couple that wants to save money continues spending frivolously. The person who wants to read better still spends five hours a day watching TV. The student who wants a better grade still spends more time holding the telephone than a book. These are all examples of people who refuse to break free from limiting patterns of behavior.

We all do a lot of things every day. The problem is that many of us do the exact same things without questioning our thoughts and behaviors. To make a change, you must look beyond your customary ways of thinking and behaving, because different action creates different results. So ask yourself, "What can I do right now that would help me move toward my desired result?" Once you identify an activity that will help you progress, do it. Just take action. Don't sit around trying to make your idea perfect before getting started. Perfection comes from experience, and experience comes from learning, right? However, learning comes from failure, and failure comes from imperfection. So, instead of spending countless of hours researching the perfect plan to get fit, just get on the treadmill and fine tune your workouts as you go along. Remember, tiny changes now mean huge results later, so any form of action in the right direction means some kind of positive change in the long run.

Though it's important to work hard at achieving your goal, it's just as, if not more, important to work intelligently. This involves focusing on "productivity" as well as production. One way to do this is to give your very best to everything you do. This means you must make a conscious, determined decision to go that "extra mile" when it comes to activities that bring you value.

Most of us know what we must do to become a top performer in a chosen field, but so few actually get around to making the transition. Why? Well, because they haven't really decided to do it. You can either get in the game or sit on the bench and watch, but either way, you must decide. Come to a conclusion, and then follow it through the best you can.

Until you take some kind of action, you will not even be sure what types of challenges you will have to face along the way. It's easy for people to get caught up in the "Thinking and Planning" stage. This is where you endlessly prepare to take action, but never get around to actually doing anything. Much of this behavior stems from the fear of failure. Perpetual planning allows a person to think that he or she is making progress, without ever having to face the challenge of making things work in real life.

Fear of letting go of what once was also holds people back from taking action. In order to take your life to the next level, you must be willing to relinquish some of your old habits, routines and ways of thinking. This idea really scares some people. If you've always done things a certain way, there will be some natural internal resistance to replacing that pattern. It's not that successful people don't feel this resistance; they simply choose to act in spite of it. You must do the same if you ever want things to improve in your life.

Perpetual preparing can become another form of procrastination. Don't let your deepest fears, worries and insecurities hold you back this way. Motivational speaker Les Brown once said, "Make your move before you're ready." You can't make sure that everything is ideal before you get started. It's better to take action and navigate through whatever challenges may arise.

Have you ever known people who incessantly put off making their move towards success? They always seem to have a "reason" for putting things off until next Monday, next week, next month or next year. These people spend eternity waiting for "the right time" and never get past the tipping point of success. At the same time, haven't you also known people who are inclined to take a good idea and just "run with it?" These types of people don't sit around waiting for things to happen. They go out and take life by the horns. You and that person may start out in similar positions, but before long, you find that he or she has far exceeded your accomplishments in a certain area. Perhaps you spent the last several years wanting to go into business for yourself, while a childhood friend of yours became an entrepreneur straight out of school. Maybe you've always wanted to write a book, and someone you know has already completed two. We all have examples like these in our lives. It can sometimes feel embarrassing to think of how others have left us so far behind. Learning of other people's success, however, should make you feel empowered, not embarrassed. These people have shown you that it is possible to create what you want if you're willing to get out there and do something. You don't have to be the smartest person in the world. You don't need a bunch of degrees, training or specialized expertise. All you need is the incredible "emotional hunger" to get out into the field and start going for what you want.

We all have the immense ability to create what we want. However, there's something important that we must all understand. We have an equal amount of power to produce both positive and negative circumstances. The "cause and effect" equation is a natural law, just like that of gravity or motion. It will not and cannot be violated. We must understand and respect this law. Ignorance of it will hurt us, even if we have the best of intentions.

If a baby crawls off the top of a tall building, it will fall to the ground and almost surely die. It doesn't matter that the baby doesn't understand the law of gravity. It makes no difference that the baby is innocent and basically good. The law respects neither person nor position; it just is. It operates in the same way for everyone, no matter who you are. This may seem obvious, but so many people try to skirt or even violate the basic law of cause and effect. One person may be tempted to grab a "fast buck" and let a con artist take him down. Another might take important advice from a good friend who has been producing bad results in her own life. There are times when you should listen to your heart, but when your feelings start to unreasonably override good judgment, you're asking for a mammoth dose of trouble. A bad decision will lead to bad results, despite how you felt when making it. Yes, you must take risks. You must be willing to venture past your comfort zone, but that is no justification for making obviously careless decisions.

People frequently do this when it comes to making money. They get so caught up in the idea of doubling or tripling their investments that they fail to build a safety net into their money-making strategy. Another area of life in which this commonly occurs is relationships. A person might get swept away by the flashy side of a potential partner and ignore "red flags" that are popping up all around.

There may be times when you begin to think, "Why should this happen to me? I do my best to be a good person." But the truth is: Why not you? Remember that the law of cause and effect doesn't make adjustments to fit the personality of each person. It is constant and unchanging. If you don't fix the holes in your roof, you're going to get leaks. It doesn't matter that you used the money intended for the roof to buy a great gift for your best friend. Perhaps buying the gift was worth it, but that's still a choice that comes with the associated consequences.

So, make sure that you remain aware of this important aspect of achievement. You must live with enthusiasm and passion, but always be thoughtful about whatever you do and conscious of the potential consequences. Know why you are making a certain choice, and be honest with yourself. It won't benefit you to rationalize decisions that are not in your best interest.

CHAPTER X:

WORKSHEET

In what parts of your life would you like to become more effective or productive?

In what ways could you adjust your normal routines to get more out of what you do?

What kind of effect would doing this have on your life?

What behavior patterns do you continue to carry out, even though you know that it would be better to do something different?

What small things could you start doing, on a regular basis, that would help you move toward your goals?

What are some time-wasting activities that you participate in during the course of a normal day?

How could you do less of these things or replace them with more useful ways of behaving?

If you work on turning these new behaviors into habits, how will your life change by next week, next month and next year?

CHAPTER XI

Operate in a Spirit of Play

Becoming successful in life is a skill, and in order to truly master any skill, you have to operate in a spirit of play. Animals play in order to practice and learn important survival skills. Think of a little kitten sneaking up on small insects, pouncing on shoes, and play-fighting with other creatures. These activities actually prepare a cat for life in the wild. Human beings operate in much the same way. Play is one of our primary means of learning. It is not only an act of entertainment, but also an important skill-building developmental process. Little children try on various roles by playing pretend. They see themselves performing in different arenas. They go beyond what is considered reasonable and let their imaginations fly into the stratosphere. Because of this, kids are immeasurably creative. Their minds have not yet been restricted by social standards. As we grow older, those in authority tell us that we should settle down, get serious and pull our heads out of the clouds. We are socialized to believe that adults work, not play, and that having certain types of fun is only for children. For this reason, many grown-ups in our society find it extremely hard to reignite the creative genius of their youth.

Work is very different from play. Work is an activity performed, despite difficulty, in hopes of gaining a future reward. Work also has a somewhat negative connotation. It assumes an obligation—a task that is not necessarily pleasurable, but must be done. Now, don't get me wrong. Work is very important and it does have a place in your life. Work can be immensely rewarding, and it can make you much stronger as a person. However, everything in life requires a balance, and unless you can get back in touch with your playful side, you will not reach the level of mastery in any endeavor.

As an example, I'm going to describe the life of one of my clients. For the sake of confidentiality, we're going to call him Thomas. Thomas is only about ten years old, but he's been in love with playing the guitar since age five. He plays music practically all of the time, day and night. Thomas wakes up especially early so that he can grab his instrument before school and strum out a few chords. During lunch, he writes songs about everything from a frog on the ground to the stars above. Because he is so passionate about his craft, Thomas has learned to make key distinctions in the quality of sound. He has gotten incredibly good at playing the guitar, and people love to hear his songs. One day, a big-time music producer gets word of Thomas's talent. He makes a special trip to meet the child and have a talk with his parents. He tells Thomas's mom and dad that their boy may soon be a great success. The producer says that by utilizing insider resources and industry contacts he can practically make Thomas an overnight sensation. Before they know it, mom and dad are signing on the bottom line. Thomas will now be making a lot of money by doing the very thing he truly loves.

However, the professional music industry ends up turning Thomas's world upside down. People are brought in to update his clothes, hair, songs and public persona. Before long, Thomas is made into a cultural icon, someone who represents the commercial idea of an industry talent. Thomas is also instructed to work very hard. He is reprimanded for his childlike fantasies, his drive to be imaginative and unique. Thomas is made to be just like other performers of his age. He is constantly driven to perform according to industry protocol. Through time, Thomas begins to lose his zest for music. He is being worked to the bone, which starts to show in his performances.

As a teenager, Thomas's life takes a detrimental turn. He begins using various drugs, trying to alter his state with whatever chemical becomes available. Eventually, Thomas goes to jail and finds himself in the middle of a media frenzy aimed at tearing him down in the public eye.

You see, Thomas started performing in a spirit of play. He was passionate, dedicated and uninhibited in his pursuit. After a while, however, music simply became work and Thomas was saddled with the pressure that accompanies obligation. Thomas was forced to become focused on meeting a preset standard, a counterfeit image of who he truly was. I was truly honored to work with Thomas at that critical stage to remind him what music really meant to him and to reignite his love for his craft.

We've all seen this kind of thing happen. A young pop star comes into view, full of energy, enthusiasm and talent, and over a short amount of time this same person steadily slips into a hole of destruction and despair. What often happens is that the person's original sense of play is shattered by the pursuit of monetary gain. What was once joy becomes nothing but a job, and there is no longer any internal motivation carrying the artist forward.

As I stated earlier, however, work also has tremendous value. In fact, nothing can take the place of hard work. In order to become successful, you will likely need to put an enormous amount of time, effort and energy toward achieving your goals. You will have to do things that make you feel uncomfortable. You must practice taking action, over and over again, until what you want comes into existence. All work and no play, though, is not the path to take because too much work without an emotional reward can kill passion and enthusiasm. You can get to be very good at something by simply working hard. To achieve mastery, however, you must allow yourself to play because play is creative in nature. It allows you to fantasize and imagine, to go beyond mainstream ideas and traditions and into areas of reality that have you have not yet seen.

Play, unlike work, is self-perpetuating. It gives us the drive to continue doing what we are involved in because play is usually performed for its own sake. It's simply a means of having fun. A playful activity is therefore instantly rewarding and continues to be so as long as you're doing it. This stimulates our internal need to move toward pleasure.

Remember, however, that work is performed in the expectation of a future reward. You must continue doing the activity for certain amount of time before any sort of benefit is received. When you play, what you're doing is looking at life as though it were an experiment. In an experiment, there is no right or wrong answer, only results. Researchers work in a spirit of curiosity. They step back and examine circumstances to see what can be found out.

You can look at your life in the same way. Experimenting with life will help you keep that sense of playfulness in your daily activities. You can strive to achieve certain things and just have fun at the same time. You can examine and interpret, without injury or fear. You can sit back and say, "That's interesting. What will happen if I do this now?" Viewing life in this way will allow you to make important distinctions that will help you become an elite performer in any field. You can enjoy the process, which makes everything you're doing worthwhile.

CHAPTER XI:

WORKSHEET

Set aside at least 10 minutes each day to dream and fantasize about achieving your goals. When thinking about your ideal life, answer these questions:

What kind of freedom do you enjoy in your ideal life?

What is your income?

What kind of relationships do you have?

How much enthusiasm do you bring to each day?

What does your body look like and how do you feel?

How do others respond to you differently, now that you have a new outlook on life?

What parts of your ideal future self haven't you yet produced today?

What kind of person have you become on the way to your dream?

Now, use these questions to gain insight into how you can put more play into your life:

What methods of play did you participate in as a child that you no longer allow yourself to engage in as an adult?

What activities did you become involved with because they were fun, but later found that the same tasks became nothing but work?

What would you pretend to be, have or do if your imagination was unrestricted now?

What types of games or recreational activities do you enjoy?

Write down some time that you can allocate each week to just having fun.

CHAPTER XII

Know How to Read the Environment

I'm very excited about discussing this next area of personal achievement. How well you understand this principle will make a huge difference in what you are able to get out of life. We're now going to talk about how to read your environment—how to interpret things that the outside world is showing you. It is crucial that you develop the ability to read your environment accurately. You must know when you're on the right course and when you need to adjust your efforts.

How will you know when you've reached your goal if you aren't aware of what things will look like once you have it? Your environment is an important indicator of how well you're doing in any area of life. There is a simple and wonderful way to assess your performance at any moment. It is the key to making distinctions between the behaviors you need to improve and those you should keep.

One way that you can receive feedback is through other people. Friends and family may have valuable insights that you can use to improve your performance. However, there are some dangers to soliciting advice from those you know. You must make sure that the person from whom you seek counsel is knowledgeable about the subject matter at hand. We human beings have a tendency to just ask anyone we know about a particular topic. Add to this the fact that people generally like giving their opinions and are often less informed about a subject than they believe, and you end up with a massive amount of misinformation that travels between friends, family and associates like wildfire.

I have a general rule when it comes to getting information from others. If they're not doing it, then they don't know it. Obviously, there are exceptions to this rule. However, a person who has wanted something for himself but has not produced it shouldn't be advising you on the subject, period. Let me pose a couple of questions: Why is it that many financial advisors are not producing wealth themselves? Wouldn't it be more advantageous to study the habits of those who have accumulated money and put their routines into practice for yourself?

You can see the "Bad Information" syndrome playing out all around you. A person who is in worse physical condition than you may try to offer fitness advice. People stuck in bad relationships seem to just love telling others how to keep a happy home. We want to trust and believe those we know, and they may truly have good intentions, which makes it even harder not to listen. If you want to enhance the quality of your life, however, you have to be selective about who and what you listen to. When people offer you advice, look at how well they're doing in the area of discussion. If they are producing positive results, then perhaps you should heed what they say. If the same part of their life is crumbling, however, you could probably let those words fly in one ear and out the other. You don't have to let anyone know that you don't believe in the value of his or her opinion. You can simply choose, in your own mind, to only follow the advice of people who have a proven record of performance.

Another reason to be selective when it comes to taking advice is that everyone has his or her own outlook on life. Each person is an individual, with his or her own unique set of values, beliefs and motives. Interpretation is often biographical in nature. When a person tells you what is or is not possible, he or she is speaking from his or her own perception of limitation. Unless you are talking to someone who has learned to be fairly objective about life, what you'll often get is a mere recount of personal experiences and superstitions.

You want to break completely away from others' inadequacies. You may desire to achieve something that nobody you've ever known has done. For this reason, it's important that you have your own internal compass, your own instinctive sense of purpose and possibility.

Another important way to gauge how well you're doing in any area of life is to look out for results. Your results will always tell you whether your thoughts, feelings and behaviors are actually producing what you want. This may seem quite obvious, but in fact many people disregard the importance of studying results.

Do you want to see how well your philosophy about relationships works? What are you producing in that area? Is the intimacy level between you and your mate increasing or diminishing? Are you living in a passionate environment, or is there an unspoken distance between you and your partner?

Say you want to start your own business. Are you moving toward that goal or away from it? Are you completing more useful activities during the day, or are you in the same exact place that you were last week, last month, last year? The answers to these questions will tell you how well your plans are working out.

We live in a world that is too caught up with opinions. Results, though, are the key to living with purpose. In any area of your life, all you have to do to find out what works and what doesn't is take a look at what you're producing. Some of us have a tendency to think that things are working out well when they're not. We all know a person who has a justification for everything that is going wrong. If he or she is not getting sales, it's because people are prejudiced or closed minded. If a child is acting out at school, it's because the teachers are being unfair. Difficulty in relationships always ends up being the other person's problem.

There may be some truth to any one of these opinions. However, this way of thinking does not allow any room for improvement. It only motivates you to stay the same and continue to reap unwanted consequences. Getting feedback from your environment is all about learning to look at your results objectively. This is sometimes hard to do, as most of us have been taught that not being right is a bad thing.

A child at school is reprimanded for having wrong answers. He or she gets back test papers filled with huge red marks. The teacher wants one particular answer, and if the child doesn't produce it, then he or she is wrong. Many children develop a huge fear of making mistakes and these fears are often carried into adulthood.

So, we are internally driven to believe that the way we're doing things is right. However, there's no shame in making mistakes. In fact, the mistakes that you make in life are your path to success. You're going to have to go through a period of learning in which you gain understanding and knowledge through experience. Difficulties and challenges are there to teach you techniques that you can use to become better and better at what you do. Learn to master this concept and you'll be well on your way to fulfilling your dreams.

CHAPTER XII:

WORKSHEET

What results are you getting right now in these areas of your life?
Relationships:

Finances:

Career:

Health:

Personal Development:

Attitude:

List some advice that you have gotten from people you knew who weren't producing quality results in their own lives.

What personal motives may some of your friends and family have for trying to steer you in a particular direction?

When have you found others projecting their limitations onto you?

What are the things that your results tell you need to be improved?

How can you use this information to move toward your goals?

CHAPTER XIII

Learn from Feedback and Adjust

Once you learn how to read the environment, it's time to make the appropriate adjustments. Having the ability to be flexible in your approach is essential to succeed in any area of your life. Your results will give you vital information about what needs to be done. There's no point in reviewing your results if you don't make it a point to use that information and change your behavior.

As I've said before, change is difficult for many people. It's much easier to just continue running the same program, following the same routine, over and over again. However, change is necessary. In order to produce something new, you just can't hold on to old ways of thinking and behaving. You can't expect to create new levels of happiness and prosperity in your life without opening yourself to change. It just won't happen.

So what you want to do is embrace those changes that support your personal development. You now know how to figure out what's working and what's not. This step is about making the bad things good and the good things even better. When you know that something is not working for you, it becomes your responsibility to take charge and correct it. No one else is going to do it for you, and your life will not transform without intervention. It's now time to go back to one of our previous chapters and "Do Something." This is the only way to get more of what you want and less of what you don't.

If you have an idea for great business, what are the first steps you can take to make it a reality? Maybe you can research grant opportunities for entrepreneurs in your area. Perhaps you can set up meetings with investors who have the ability to put capital toward your dream. If your relationship is suffering, you may not have some information that you need. You could read a book on communication or check out relationship seminars posted online. The important thing is that you make the adjustments, that you see what needs improving and take immediate action.

Your goal is your final destination and the feedback you receive is your compass that tells you whether you're on course. However, you alone are responsible for getting back on the path to personal achievement. It would do no good for you to see your weaknesses and do absolutely nothing to improve them.

Life rarely happens in a straight line. The path you have chosen will likely twist and turn several times before you produce the results you want. Adjustments will need to be made—that's a fact. Whether you succeed will largely be determined by how well you can roll with the punches. Just think of someone who's driving an automobile through traffic. This person has to constantly navigate spontaneous changes that occur in the environment. He or she has to be aware of traffic signals, signs, the vehicle's temperature, speed and distance, and the movement of other travelers. Your life operates in much the same way. Things can come at you from any angle, at any time. You alone are responsible for modifying your approach in a way that keeps you moving towards your target destination. The person who fails to observe changes in traffic will crash. Likewise, you will smash into every obstacle that pops up unless you learn to move over and around them.

There's a saying that goes, "When you find yourself in a hole, stop digging!" When you notice that something's not working, stop and do something else. It's that simple. Many people are led by their egos. They don't want to admit that the first attempt at doing something wasn't perfect, that there were flaws in their original plan. However, this is not a sensible way to go about getting what you want. You're looking for a result, not an ego boost. You want to create a higher quality of life, not pat yourself on the back at all times. Nobody who made it big did so without making some adjustments. Look into the stories of successful people and you'll see that this is true.

Real estate billionaire Donald Trump went complete broke at one time. He lost everything he had, yet he was still able to come back and create even greater results than he had created before. In fact, most millionaires and successful business people have gone bankrupt two or three times, but they took each loss as a chance to gain experience and knowledge. They made adjustments and eventually got to the desired result. So why should you think that life will lay out the red carpet for you? Why would you believe that your path would not enter some rocky terrain? Trust me, it will, but you are much greater than whatever challenges may come about. You have the power to figure things out along the way. Embrace this concept and you will have taken a huge step toward achieving your goals. A person can try to escape the necessity of changing his or her behavior by making excuses or rationalizing away his or her results, but using this approach merely ensures that nothing different will happen. Nothing will change, until you do. You can't avoid making adjustments if you genuinely intend to improve your life. The ability to "bounce back" from adversity is one of the most important characteristics you can develop. When something happens that you don't like, you simply can't afford to sit around and throw a "pity party" for yourself. If you suffer a significant loss, like the death of a loved one, you may need to grow through some sort of mourning period, and that's perfectly natural. However, remember that you can't mourn forever. Heartache knocks on everyone's door at some point. As long as you're still here, it means your life must go on.

If you can imagine doing better in any area of life, then it is your responsibility to make that vision become real. Excuses don't count. All the energy it takes to formulate and keep up with rationalizations can be used to figure out and make the appropriate adjustments. There's always something you can do, even if it's a very, very little something.

For example, what if getting started down the path toward what you want requires a lot of money that you don't have? Try thinking about the issue in a new way. You don't have to get every commodity you need by direct purchase. Lots of commerce in today's market is done through barter—trading goods you have or services you can perform for those you need. Some people use this method to acquire most of their material needs. You can also raise capital by getting investors involved with your projects. You may not have the money, but somebody does. There are lots of organizations that look to help bring funding to people with good ideas. Of course, an investor may expect a portion of any potential profits in return, but this may be a useful avenue for you if what you have to offer is worth it.

When you face something that seems like an obstacle, you must use what you have to get around, over or through it. When a football or basketball team goes into half time losing the game, the players don't return running the same routine. The other squad may be faster or stronger or better in some areas, but the losing team can't let any of this determine how the game will end. They must make adjustments by using what they have to overcome whatever challenges exist.

Challenges are often life's way of presenting you with an opportunity to grow. Really successful people push beyond tough times. They make it an ultimate priority to realize the dreams and goals that they have set for themselves. These people have simply decided that whatever obstacles arise will not stand in their way.

There are two types of obstacles, internal and external. External obstacles include things like lack of resources, lack of contacts and so on. Internal obstacles are things like personal insecurities, self-doubt and disempowering stories about one's abilities. More often than not, the internal barriers are what really prevent us from moving forward. As mentioned earlier, there is almost always a way to get past material obstacles. The limits of your own perception, however, can be much more difficult to overcome.

One thing that makes this true is the human tendency to believe one's own interpretations. Suppose you held a belief that you needed lots of money to get ahead. In your mind, that idea wouldn't be a belief; it would be a fact. You would then dismiss evidence to the contrary and end up missing out on countless opportunities. So, part of receiving feedback involves getting your mental game in order. You must begin to see even your own thoughts and beliefs as things that can be changed and improved. Remember that ideas are inside of your head. They may not necessarily exist in the outside world. In order to receive worthwhile feedback, you must be willing to take on a highly objective view of your habits, thoughts and surroundings.

CHAPTER XIII:

WORKSHEET

What do you perceive needs improvement in each of these areas of life?

Relationships:

Finances:

Career:

Health:

Personal Development:

Attitude:

What could you do to improve the problems in each area? Make sure each alternative is aimed at resolving a specific condition. For example, if your spouse believes that you don't listen enough, just saying "I love you" more won't help the situation. Instead, you might need to practice active listening and more effective communication strategies. Don't get in the habit of putting most of your effort towards things that don't address the issue at hand. That is a sure way to remain stuck in problematic patterns.

Below, write some ways that you can modify your behavior to get a better result in each area.
Relationships:

Finances:

Career:

Health:

Personal Development:

Attitude:

List some things you've recently done that produced less-than-desirable results for you.

How could you go about these tasks differently next time to give yourself a greater chance of creating an outcome that is closer to ideal?

Do you recognize the need for change in certain areas of your life, yet find yourself refusing to alter your approach?

What beliefs do you need to adopt in order to become more flexible?

CHAPTER XIV

Persist

Now we're stepping up the big leagues. You have almost everything in place to create massive positive results in your life. You made a plan, you took action and you made appropriate adjustments. Now, you must be unrelenting in the pursuit of your goals.

Success and failure are often separated by determination. The difference between people who merely dream of doing great things and those who don't is persistence.

Persistence will take you places that talent alone cannot. A part of being persistent is being proactive. You may not have people lining up to offer you opportunities. Perhaps you don't come from a wealthy family and lack the financial backing needed to get your business started, so you will have to make many of your own breaks in life. You will often be required to create an opening where none exists. You can't wait around for ideal conditions to emerge. You must approach your dreams with a take-charge attitude.

Remember when we discussed "Getting into the Right Spot"? A persistent person positions himself or herself for success. He or she wakes up before other people to get a head start on the day. He or she studies instead of watching celebrity gossip. He or she volunteers before being asked and doesn't run away from those rare opportunities that do fall into his or her lap. That inner conversation that goes on within all of our minds often encourages us to hold back. It says, "You're not ready yet. Practice some more and we'll go after the next one." However, the persistent person knows how to shut that voice down. He or she says, "I'm going to go ahead and do it anyhow." He takes a leap of faith, knowing that nothing can knock his or her "foolproof mentality" off course.

So, I want you to learn to embrace the challenges that come your way. Great things can come out of what seems like a terrible situation. Have you ever had something happen to you in the past that you thought was bad, but later learned that it was a blessing in disguise? Going through hard times may improve the quality of your character or make you stronger as a person. In order to grow, you must be willing to move through some degree of discomfort. This is true no matter if your goal is physical, emotional or mental. As you probably know, a muscle must be pushed beyond its normal limits to grow stronger, and so does your emotional fitness when it comes to achieving your growth goals. When you begin to take on a new set of ideas and beliefs, you're going to experience some psychological resistance. This could take the form of confusion, self-doubt, discouraging thoughts or a host of other negative mental conditions. Even though it may be frustrating to experience these things, doing so can actually be a good thing. Having these types of reactions means you're about to stretch your boundaries. You're right there at the edge of growth. It's just like that feeling you get by lifting weights and going for three or four more repetitions than normal. That mental disruption is the "burn," that mental fatigue that's going to lead you into greater and stronger thought processes. The same thing is likely to happen when you make an effort to achieve some type of emotional growth. Whether you are attempting to become calmer, more confident, and more cheerful or loving, some pretty weird things are likely to come up.

The interesting thing is that you may experience a swell of feelings that on the surface may seem to have nothing to do with your original goal. When you attempt to become more confident, for instance, you may start experiencing an unexpected rush of loneliness from time to time. When your goal is to become calmer and more even-headed, a sense of heartbreak might come your way. There's no need to feel discouraged or fearful when this happens. That emotional turbulence is telling you that you're entering a period of transition, that you're shaking things up one last time before moving on. I have no way of telling you exactly what those kinds of feelings could mean. Maybe that lack of confidence was simply a way to avoid leaving your usual crowd behind. Now you feel lonely at the thought of moving on. Maybe your anger was a way to cover up some hurt that you experienced long ago and now you're finally feeling the pain. What I do know about those emotions for sure, though, is that they are essential to your growth.

Challenges can be good for growth because they push you out of your comfort zone. If you're always comfortable, then you're probably only doing that which you already know. Despite popular belief, it's hard to learn much if things work out well for you all of the time. Tribulation has the power to spark creative genius, however, because it forces you to look for, explore and develop new solutions. You may feel like quitting sometimes, and that's normal. Just remind yourself that whatever troubles you're facing will eventually pass. All you have to do is pull yourself up by your bootstraps and keep going. Ignore negative people and circumstances. Disregard distractions, and know that you will eventually get what you want. Trust in the process and stick with it, because doing so gives you the power to produce massive results in your life.

The only question is "Are you willing to make it happen?" Are you ready to do what you need to over and over again, learning, growing and experimenting until what you want comes into your life? You don't want to look back at the end of your life and know that you could've done more. The discomfort you encounter on the way to your goals is much easier to stomach than the pain of regret. The persistent person is not afraid to run one more mile, read one more book, or knock on one more door. He doesn't feel guilty about calling the head of a major corporation and asking for business. He would be more disappointed if he did not try, if he did not make the effort to get something more out of life. Don't fear moving forward; fear going backwards. Don't worry about what others will say if you do it. Worry about what you will say to yourself if you don't. Even emotions that we call negative have a purpose. Use them to energize you, revitalize you, and allow you to get much more out of what you do.

Being persistent also helps to build confidence. You begin to learn that problems will eventually fall before you if you just keep going. After a while, it can become a game to see how many different angles you'll have to take to get something before victory is yours. Remember when you were a child and adults would reprimand you for being stubborn? Little did they know that the very same quality would be required for you to become successful. When you are going after a better life, you must become incredibly stubborn about making it work. Often things would go our way if we were just willing to push a little bit harder. Think about this. Isn't it true that it is very likely that you won't do something very well the first time that you try it? This goes for learning practically everything, from walking and talking to reading and writing. Isn't getting what you want worth going through those initial stages of trial and error? If it is, then you must develop the quality of persistence.

As long as you keep learning and gaining experience, you are on the right path. As long as you watch what's going on and make the appropriate adjustments, things will be all right. Don't just try one thing. You may have to adopt ten, twenty or a hundred different approaches before you find the one that suits your need. Tony Robbins says, "Success in life is the result of good judgment. Good judgment is usually the result of experience. Experience is usually the result of bad judgment." Can you see how the number of attempts you make is not important? What matters is that you keep going until the objective is met. In fact, those little bumps that line your chosen path are a part of your journey to success. Without taking a few bumps on the head, you wouldn't develop the qualities you need to become the type of person who has what you want.

If you want to find the perfect mate, for instance, you'll have to gain some experience with talking to people and becoming the kind of person that you want to attract. If you want to be a great schoolteacher, you must acquire tools that enable you to engage young minds. You'll almost surely experience some discomfort during the first stages of developing any new skill. That is why in any area of life only a select few people do really well. They are the ones who refuse to give up, who stubbornly persevere in spite of difficulty. This means that you must open yourself to taking risks. Most people like to stay with what's safe, with what they already know, but that type of mentality eliminates the potential for growth and discovery. In addition, lots of people stop short before reaching success because they don't believe they will be able to survive the challenges that lie ahead. For instance, a person who wants to change careers may feel fearful of losing her livelihood. A person who wants to get out of some toxic relationship may believe that no one else will ever love him. These types of fears are not to be taken lightly. They are real to the person who feels them, and it is very hard for someone to move forward while shackled to such ideas. However, as former President of the United States Theodore Roosevelt once said, "It is hard to fail, but it is worse never to have tried to succeed." The difficulties you may face on your path to personal achievement are indeed real, but even more real are the difficulties that will arise if you don't make the transition. See, setbacks can always be overcome, but the pain of regret never loses its sting.

You may feel as though you will be letting others down if you don't succeed, but by not expressing your true greatness, you are doing them a much greater disservice. Only by becoming free to take the risks that lead to personal achievement can you truly make yourself an asset to the world around you. You will likely fall at least a few times before reaching your goal. But, as I've heard many times, "Success can build character, but failure reveals it." Your mistakes and mishaps provide important feedback that is essential to your growth, understanding and development. Something that seems difficult right now may be preparing you for great future success. So you need to view everything that happens to you as a learning experience.

Yes, we all feel fearful from time to time, but most people make the mistake of believing that being afraid is a valid reason to not take action. Nothing could be further from the truth. We are all human and, in certain contexts, fear is a very natural human experience, but you can learn to master and harness this emotion for your greater good by utilizing it as a motivator. For example, the fear of being insignificant might motivate you to go out and make a different in the world. The fear of being a failure can cause you to stick to your guns when times are hard. The fear of being unfulfilled may inspire you to take a wonderful "leap of faith" toward your goals. The bottom line is that fear does not justify inactivity. Just because you're scared to do something doesn't mean that you shouldn't do it. In fact, that fear probably identifies an area that you need to explore or work on. Remember that both the body and mind are very wise. Immeasurable potentialities flow through every cell and fiber of your being. When you know you should take a particular action but feel afraid to do so, it means you are standing at the edge of a new and promising reality. You are on the verge of making a tremendous and powerful breakthrough.

CHAPTER XIV:

WORKSHEET

Gold medalist and civil rights advocate Bill Bradley once said, "Ambition is the path to success. Persistence is the vehicle you arrive in." What do you think he meant by this?

How does this insight apply to your own life?

Remember your big "WHY." Explain why your purpose is big enough to move you past any obstacles that come up.

List some like-minded people who you can begin to associate with and go to for encouragement when times get hard.

What potential distractions should you force your mind to ignore right now?

Which of your chosen tasks might you possibly be underestimating the difficulty of?

What steps can you take to ready yourself for added stresses that might arise?

Why is it important for you to follow through in pursuit of your goals?

What pain results from not following through?

How will you maintain your determination when a certain approach seems to fail?

CHAPTER XV

Secondary Gain

One thing to watch out for is secondary gain. Secondary gain is an indirect benefit derived from an often unwanted difficulty. It comes about when a person's subconscious mind believes that having the problem helps to meet some deeper emotional need. If the person tries to change, she is internally driven to remain the same.

Three years ago, I got a call from a client, a young mother, who was complaining about frequent migraine headaches. The pain she felt was excruciating, and it left her powerless to undertake everyday responsibilities. She told me she had already gone to the doctor and discovered the true nature of her problem. She'd had an infected wisdom tooth that was agitating nerves connected through the head. After having the tooth pulled, the woman encountered a surprising turn of events. She was pain-free for about two weeks, but then the migraines returned, stronger than ever. Medical professionals were baffled at the woman's condition. They could find no organic reason for the headaches and were at a complete loss to explain this phenomenon. However, when we took a deeper look into her life, the cause of her relapse became apparent. Since having had a child, the woman had been working herself to the bone. She always seemed to be doing something and had no time at all for personal interests or pursuits. In fact, she often felt like nothing more than a machine, a tool to take care of others' needs. She was treated very differently when she had a migraine attack, however. People actually cared about how she felt and attended to her needs. In a strange way, the headaches helped her feel appreciated by others, like a person instead of a machine. Once the migraines were gone, the woman's subconscious mind feared that she would also lose that ability to feel valued and cherished. It therefore brought the headaches back to ensure that this wouldn't happen. As strange as that might seem, the pain was real, yet the minute we "deprogrammed" this learning, the pain magically disappeared because the subconscious mind understood that the irrational pain was no longer serving its purpose.

Human beings are goal-driven. This means everything we do is for a reason. Remember that every mental program is driven by the "emotion and experience" sequence. Even unproductive patterns of behavior are set up in the effort to gain some perceived benefit. If you want to change an aspect of your life, know how to do so, but are still falling short, then there may be an issue of secondary gain hiding beneath the surface.

In that case, ask yourself, "What have I been getting out of this destructive pattern of behavior? In what ways have I been benefiting from the problem?" When you can answer these questions, you will be able to create a conscious strategy for breaking those unwanted associations. Secondary gain is like a gremlin roaming around in the darkness, sabotaging your best efforts from behind the scenes. You want to get rid of any hidden beliefs that keep you stuck to a problem and replace them with ones that allow you to advance. Your subconscious mind will do whatever it takes to keep you from suffering a perceived loss. The problem is that the road to success often requires moving through pain. Sometimes the right thing to do is not the one that feels good in the moment. Your subconscious mind does not have the capacity to reason. It doesn't know that facing the fear of uncertainty now can lead you to overwhelming joy in the future. It simply works to move you away from pain and toward pleasure at any time. A common side effect of the subconscious's desire for secondary gain—one most of us are familiar with—is procrastination.

Procrastination is often just a tool used by the subconscious to keep you away from something that it believes will be painful. For one thing, procrastination keeps you from taking risks and becoming disappointed if things don't work out. It also protects you from being overwhelmed by managing the potential pressure of success. Your inner mind may view the toils of achievement as unnecessary pain.

When you recognize the role that secondary gain plays in your life, you can work at finding alternative measures to satisfy your emotional needs. If you find ways to excel at what you do and still get the feelings you need, you will take a major step in rewiring your brain for success. Your brain will accept a better option if one is available. You don't need to become ill for people to care about you. Instead, start reaching out to others. Become a person of compassion, empathy and understanding. Project goodwill towards others and you will receive it in return. Don't procrastinate to avoid failure. Prepare for setbacks; expect them to come. Develop a strong "WHY" and let it move you past anything that pops up. Spend time learning about your chosen task. Build confidence by developing your skill set. The more information you have going in, the less frightening that first step is likely to be. You can take a similar approach toward eliminating the fear of success. As you seek to improve the quality of your life, things will change. You will be required to step out onto unfamiliar ground to reach a higher level of performance. You must accept full responsibility for both your choices and consequences. Instead of fearing these changes, however, you can embrace them. Remember what we discussed about getting curious and experimenting with life. Looking at things this way will turn anxiety into excitement and worry into enthusiasm. This will give your brain an incentive for moving forward instead of discouraging it.

Next, you need to practice these new behaviors. Make a habit of meeting your emotional needs in more resourceful ways. When you find genuine ways of getting what you want, your brain will have no need to sabotage your efforts.

CHAPTER XV:

WORKSHEET

Write down an area of your life that you want to change and have tried to change, but don't seem to make any progress in.

What could you be getting out of continuing this pattern?

How has seeking to fill your needs in this way affected your life up until now?

What are some more useful ways that you could experience those same emotions?

When you find better ways to meet your emotional needs, how will your life change this week?

This month?

This year?

If you don't substitute your destructive behaviors, what will you get out of life this week?

This month?

This year?

PART IV: GAINING MOMENTUM

CHAPTER XVI

Enjoy the Process

Throughout life, we all come up with sets of ideas—rules, if you will—that dictate how the world is supposed to work. Built into that concept is a person's evaluation of what he or she needs to do in order to succeed or be happy. The problem that arises is that many of us learn to create very narrow and limiting definitions of success that are impossible to live up to.

Take, for instance, the mother who decides she will be happy only when all of her kids are out of college and married. There are a few things inherently wrong with this idea. First, she has placed her ability to be happy outside of herself, dependent on the choices of others. She cannot control her children and doesn't know if any of them will even want to marry or continue education after high school.

Some people associate success with material possessions. They think, "Once I've earned 50,000, 100,000 or 1,000,000 dollars, things will be all right." The problem with this way of thinking is that money alone rarely solves money problems. People often assume—mistakenly, mind you—that all their worries would disappear if only a few more bucks would come into the coffers. But internal barriers are what mostly stop people from achieving financial independence. It's really a mindset issue, not a financial one.

If your thoughts are pulling you down into hardship, then no amount of money will ever make things better. So, if a person is addicted to either of the aforementioned definitions of success, then he or she is destined for a lifetime of disappointment. We need to play the success game in a way that works for us, one in which we make the rules and set ourselves up to win. In fact, one of the things that you most need to do to become highly successful is break out of the limits of old definitions.

The mother in our previous example who relies on her children for happiness might never get there. Instead, she could decide to govern her life by a more empowering set of rules. She might say, "I choose to fulfill myself and be happy right now. Because of this, I can encourage my children to find their own definitions of success."

The person with money problems could say, "You know, I've got a lot to be thankful for. I'm happy, alive and motivated to create even greater things in my life. Let's see how I can make this next year even better than the last." This is not to say that you should blind yourself to whatever potential challenges, but you can choose to feel successful—to feel happy—right now, where you are, with what you have.

Sometimes we can become so absorbed in a problem that we simply forget about all of the things we have to feel happy about. Don't let this happen to you. No matter what's going on in your life, you have some things to be happy about. Really think about this and take pride in recognizing those things in your life that are going well. I've said this before and I'll say it again: Everyone has something to be thankful for.

Being happy about a certain part of your life means that you perceive an alignment between your definitions and your experience. In short, you have decided that what you have produced matches or supports the way that you think things should be. Now, we want to bring this principle into other areas of your life.

So, just imagine what would happen if you were to connect your happiness to progress instead of perfection. You can never really be perfect, right? But measuring your accomplishments by the amount of progress you make gives you the opportunity to enjoy ever-increasing levels of happiness. All you have to think about is doing better than you are doing right now. You can get even a little better at anything, almost instantly. However, the major part of getting this right, of making this principle work for you, lies in developing a set of rules that allow you to be happy with whatever you possess in any moment. Then, you will be on the fast track to success.

In order to do that, you must redefine the roles that create pain for you. Any one of us will always be doing well in some areas and not so well in others. But here's the million-dollar question: What are you focusing on? Do you spend too much time thinking about what you don't have or haven't accomplished yet? Of course, it's great to have a goal and notice the difference between where you are and where you want to be, but you can't make much progress if you walk around picking at yourself all day.

Let's say that you want to learn a new language and you've given yourself three months to do it. You might be reminded of a friend who learned French in that amount of time and suppose that you will do the same. You figure that you are as, if not more, intelligent than this other person, so three months should be more than enough time. For some reason, however, you don't pick up the language as quickly. You have trouble memorizing phrases and getting the verb agreements in order. After five months, you're not even close to speaking fluently. You feel stupid, incompetent and frustrated by your apparent failure at mastering another language. Soon, you give up, feeling less sure about your intelligence and abilities.

But let's look at this problem from a different perspective. Is it really a bad thing to have not learned a complete language in just three months? Many people live for years in a foreign country before learning to speak the language well. Furthermore, your friend may have had an upper hand when it came to learning languages. It doesn't necessarily have anything to do with intelligence. He may be a highly auditory learner and simply learn things well by hearing them over and over again. He may have listened to audio recordings of French while driving, working and doing household chores. You, on the other hand, may not have the same inclination. Learning a new language, in your case, might require several months of reading and intensive study. But you've set a rigid time frame for yourself that doesn't allow for individual differences—and it's that disparity, between where you are and where you believe that you should be, which causes the pain. After three months, you may have learned a great deal of French, more than almost everyone you know. But if you're caught up in your "shoulds," you might never appreciate this fact. Some people think that the truth is painful. It can be, but it's probably more accurate to say that resistance to the truth is the real pain.

Many times, you don't suffer because of what happens. You suffer because you hold on to the thought that something else "should" be happening. One person says, "I've been trying to give up eating chocolate for three weeks now and, in that time, I've cheated four times. I'm a failure." Another person says, "I've been working on taking chocolate out of my diet for just three weeks, and in that time I've only had four pieces. I'm doing great!"

So, it's all about changing the way you evaluate progress. You don't want to kid yourself and believe that you're doing better than you are. But you also don't want to create the opposite situation where you exaggerate your faults and put yourself down on a regular basis.

When you believe you can only get things like love, respect, appreciation and self worth by conforming to some rigid ideal, you're setting yourself up to experience major distress. It's good to have an end goal, but things don't always play out the way that we plan them. Anyone who has lived on earth for even a moderate amount of time knows this to be true.

Don't we see this happening in everyday life? Don't you know someone who has a lot going for him or her, but just can't feel good about anything he or she does? Maybe you, yourself, are familiar with this type of experience. We often can be fooled into thinking that one ideal is "the key" to happiness and self-fulfillment. But, truth be told, happiness is what you need to find *first*—it is what enables you to reach higher and higher levels of achievement.

In order to reach the greatest levels of achievement, it's essential to learn to enjoy the process. You must get a sense of pleasure out of what you do. You want to feel compelled, driven to succeed. Without a sense of enjoyment, life becomes bland and drab. You want to wake up each day feeling excited and ready to take life on. Find the moment-by-moment reward in whatever it is that you do. Take pride in sharpening the fine aspects of your craft. The journey is often just as or even more fulfilling than the destination. You only go around once, so you might as well have a great time.

Why hold yourself back? There's nothing to gain by walking through life with a frown on your face. You don't get any bonus points by being cynical and negative. You're all you've got, and if you're not happy, what's the point of it all?

The key is to keep the end result in focus, but stay conscious of what's going well in the moment. See, if you spend too much time in the future, you'll be constantly reminded of how far you still have to go. The watched pot never boils. You don't want to get caught up in the "I'll be happy when…" trap. This is a mindset in which you walk around believing "I'll be happy when: I get the car I want—I get married—I get a promotion—or I have, get or accomplish anything else."

You can be happy where you are, with what you have, right now. The key is to live in a spirit of gratitude. You can't be grateful and disappointed with life at the same time. One of the secrets to being happy every day is to always remember what you have to be thankful for. This is part of what it means to control your focus, as we talked about earlier.

And all of us have things to be grateful for. Are you disappointed because there's not enough money in your bank account? If you have any money in there at all, you're already doing better than most people in the world. Perhaps you want a better car than the one you've got. That's okay, but think about this: you have a car and lots of people don't. Beyond that, you're alive. You have the power to create a new destiny starting right now. It's not over for you yet, and that could be the greatest thing to appreciate of all. You can have all the potential in the world, but you'll still self-destruct if you don't learn to control your emotions. Just being intelligent, gifted or privileged doesn't guarantee success. It's all about getting the most out of each and every day while enjoying the process of living! Am I making any sense?

CHAPTER XVI:

WORKSHEET

Why is it important to make happiness a priority in life?

Up until now, have you practiced making being happy a daily goal?

Do you take time each day to do things that give you pleasure?

If you were to make a specific plan for enjoying your life right now, what would it include?

What tasks could you accomplish this week that would give you a sense of satisfaction?

Commit to completing one or two of the abovementioned activities this week. Write down exactly what you'll do to get the job done.

What are some of your strengths, some of the things you're really good at?

How can you apply these skills further to make them work better for you in pursuit of your goals?

What's really great about you? What parts of your personality can you really feel good about?

CHAPTER XVII

Raising Your Bar – Bettering Your Best

Reaching your goal is not a single accomplishment, but a series of individual triumphs. On the way to success, you'll be required to break through many barriers and overcome many obstacles. Each essential step is about personal growth and discovery. You must consistently strive to do your best and, then, make your best even better. This is how the great ones of our era have gotten to where they are.

Think of a beginning weightlifter. He doesn't walk right into a gym and pick up 450 pounds on the first day of training. He starts with something small, say 150 pounds. He'll keep lifting that weight until it becomes easy to do so. He then moves up to 175 pounds and does the same thing. As time goes on, the weightlifter incrementally increases his workload, going from 175 to 200, to 225, and so on. After months of doing this, he accomplishes the original goal of lifting 450 pounds.

Each move up in weight was a definite win. With every advance, the lifter became "more" as an athlete. He turned into someone who was stronger, more resilient and more capable. However, the weightlifter made a point of not staying in one place too long. He knew that a big achievement is simply the combined effect of smaller victories, and that no one battle wins the war.

There will be time to celebrate, of course. When you reach a new level of achievement, it's natural to feel great about it and pat yourself on the back, but don't allow any single conquest to diminish your drive. The position that you've moved to is a new plateau. Now it's time to do something different. It's very important for you to keep looking forward. The fact that you're alive today means that you have more work to do. Have you ever noticed that certain elderly members of society will die right after a significant event takes place, like a one-hundredth birthday party or the birth of a great-grandchild? Some say that these people have a strong desire to stay around for the special occasion. Once the event has passed, however, their will to live any longer simply fades away.

Here's the thing: if you're not moving forward, then you're going backwards. Now, don't get mad at me for throwing such an old cliché at you. Those words are very true and here's why. The world is constantly evolving, moving from one level of understanding to the next. If you're not growing with it, then you're losing ground by default. You can refuse to advance, but there's really no such thing as staying in one place. What seems like stillness is simply a decline that is too gradual for you to recognize.

Don't get caught up talking to people too much about what you used to do. This is a brand new day and you've got a lot more to give. Do you find that some of your childhood friends still continuously talk about the same things that they used to years ago? It's okay to reminisce, but it's sad to see someone who's simply stuck in the past. Your life should become richer and more versatile as you get older.

People become better at things with practice, right? Wrong. Practicing the same thing in the same way won't make you any better than you already are. This is what happens to many people we know. They practice the same behaviors, think the same thoughts and tell themselves the same stories, over and over again.

I've never met anyone who spent all day walking in reverse. This is because it's usually more important to look at where you're going than where you're coming from. Take time to learn from a mistake, but once you have the lesson, let it go and move on. Some people spend way too much time focused on what happened in the past. If you make a small mistake that doesn't hurt anybody, why does it really matter? It doesn't. It's not in the slightest bit important and doesn't affect the outcome of your life in any way.

You need to think about now and where you're going from here. It doesn't do you any good to obsessively hold on to parts of your personal history that slow your growth. This goes for both positive and negative events. Looking at what you did well in the past can actually inspire you to do better. But don't lean on your victories like a crutch. Though your past actions have brought you to where you are right now, it's what you do today that determines the quality of your life tomorrow. So you have to be diligent at keeping pace. In fact, accomplishing one goal should make you hungrier than ever before because doing so lets you know that even more is possible. If you make $2,000 in one week, $3,000 becomes very doable. When you've already shed twenty-five pounds, dropping five more seems like child's play. Those little victories along the way prepare you to accomplish something much larger in the end.

When you accomplish something, however, and have nowhere else to go, life loses its zeal. You want to keep a goal in front of you, something to shoot for. If you've achieved your monetary goals, it may be time to enjoy a life of contribution. Perhaps you would find immense joy in the pursuit of improving your local community. Once you finally get the job of your dreams, focus on what you can do to create more value in that position. You've worked much too hard to simply go through the motions.

Bettering your best means that you're not competing with anyone else. Your only opponent is you. Too many people get caught up in the rat race, the idea that success is all about beating out other people. But thinking that way can often work against you. The "I win and you lose" mentality puts your focus on outcomes. In this case, the outcome is being better than everybody else. There are several problems with this outlook. First of all, how do you even quantify what "better" means? Pretty much everyone is better at something than somebody. If you operate your life from this perspective, you might feel like a failure every time someone comes up with a new approach that works. You don't know everything and you're not going to be the most talented in every area all of the time. That is why it's important for you to live by your own standards instead of comparing your accomplishments to those of other people. Another problem with thinking that you always have to win is that it puts you in a continuous state of anxiety. You can't step back and enjoy life if you're always afraid of losing your spot. People who are addicted to competition often become paranoid and start to lose trust in other people. I don't know about you, but that's not the type of life that I'd want for myself. I want to feel good, to relax and enjoy the scenery, and to love myself for just being me. That's what real success is all about.

Every time American soul legend James Brown was asked which of his performances he thought his best was, he always gave the same response: "My last one." See, James Brown was never in competition with anyone else. He was always bettering his own best. He didn't stand around and think, "Well, I've made it. Now I'm here to stay." He was always setting new milestones to go after, new targets to aim for. As a result, each performance he gave was better than all others before it.

If you look to surpass your own achievements, you'll become much better at what you do than you would by focusing on other people. Using successful people as models can work very well for you, of course. But, if you really want to become great, there's a point when you must take the reins. You can learn things from other people and take those lessons with you through life, but you also have to put something into the pot. You're here to make your own contribution.

Not many people are willing to involve themselves in a program of personal development. They'll spend more time watching sporting events and celebrity gossip on TV than they will on improving some crucial area of life. But if you really want to succeed in life, if you want to experience true happiness and fulfillment, you must make it a point to work on yourself.

Developing yourself gives you the power to change both your circumstances and your life. Think about this. The decisions that you make in any moment are a reflection of the understanding and level of awareness that you possess at the time. As you learn, evolve and grow, these aspects of your personality expand. Your ability to make different and better choices increases to the same degree. Lots of people fear self-development because it puts them back in the driver's seat. When you work on yourself, it means you recognize your power to improve the situation. For many, letting things stay the way they are and believing that circumstances are unchangeable is easier than taking responsibility to do better. But you can't embrace this lackadaisical attitude if you want to enjoy a higher quality of life. Essentially, participating in a regular regimen of self-development activities allows you to become more as a person. When you become more, you become *capable* of more—and that's it. Life can be difficult, and problems can sometimes seem too enormous to manage. But the key to success doesn't lie in wishing for your current troubles to diminish, it's about you becoming so big that they simply fall away.

Of course, this process is ongoing. As you move into the next stage of growth, there will be new challenges to face, boundaries to surpass and milestones to reach. Look at the difficulties you encounter not as things to fear, but as opportunities to build a better set of skills. You will likely find improving yourself to be both an interesting and exhilarating process.

When you become better at performing your chosen craft, for instance, you might feel compelled to find out what else there is to know. As you see yourself making a difference, it encourages you to keep going. That's why many people who get involved with self-improvement quickly become lifelong advocates.

It's very hard to feel good about yourself when you aren't doing what you're truly capable of. It's painful to live without using your true potential. Lots of people mask this pain with a combination of distractions, things like hyperactivity, alcohol, drugs, television and empty chatter. But the relief brought on by these things is just an illusion. The person inside still longs to soar, to bring forth that which he or she was designed to create.

Take one concert out of this year's event schedule and use the money you save to attend a seminar on your area of interest. Instead of registering for the newest tabloid subscription, buy a book that will help you become better at producing what you want. Take an hour out of each day's TV time and write out ways you can do things better. What's inside of you needs your help to come out. If you see an area where things can or must be improved, there is a reason that you made that observation. Maybe you're supposed to make that change, fill that need. Not everyone can see where improvements are necessary in that area, but you can.

No matter how obvious the need for change may seem to you, plenty of other people just won't "get it" because that realization was given to *you*. It is your vision, not theirs! Now the question is: What are you going to do about it? Anybody can just gripe and complain from a distance. It doesn't take any heart to silently think about the way things "should" be. Anyone can walk by a negative situation and talk about how things should be better. But you are a different kind of person. The fact that you're reading this book means that you're ready to produce some fantastic things in your life. Your job, therefore, is to speak up, to contribute and let your brilliance shine. There's no reason for you to keep your insights locked away in solitude. Now is the time to make a difference. The person who separates his or her self from the pack is the one who says, "I'll do it."

There's a saying in the sales industry: "In every interaction, somebody is sold." This means either the salesperson sells a prospect on the value of his product, or the potential client sells the vendor on his excuses not to buy. This also happens whenever you encounter challenges in life. Are you selling yourself on your potential, or your doubts? Are you giving into your passions or your fears? It takes just as much effort and energy to focus on doing well as it does to live a life of discontent. So you might as well give yourself the upper hand and bring out the powerful side of your personality.

CHAPTER XVII:

WORKSHEET

What are some of the things you've done really well over the last week, month and year?

What are some areas in which you may have performed poorly over that same period of time?

How can you enhance your strengths to improve your overall performance?

What can you do to improve your performance in areas in which you did poorly before?

What are some schools of thought that you can draw from to become better at what you do?

What skills could you develop or what training could you get that would help you achieve your goals?

Do you believe you're at a plateau in any areas of your life?

How can you modify your normal routines in a way that pushes you past your comfort zone in these areas?

CHAPTER XVIII

Giving Back

The next thing I want to talk about is the concept of giving back. Contribution is one of the little-known secrets to achievement and self-mastery. Giving back takes you into a spiritual place where you rise above material existence and enter a world where we are all one. In fact, generosity is the antidote to greed. Greed is an intense, persistent state of selfishness. A greedy person has an excessive desire to gain more than his or her fair share. He wants his, yours and everyone else's piece of the pie. Greed is an insidious disorder that deteriorates a person's character and personality from the inside out.

No one is an island. We get, enjoy and have access to things through other people. Society is all about people living, learning and creating together. However, in today's world, we're often taught to believe in a "me" versus "you," or "us" versus "them," system. We crawl into our own little bubbles and condition ourselves to disregard those we don't know. In fact, however, we are all part of the same living, flowing system. Each of us is a very important piece of this great big puzzle and deserves to be treated as such. There's an old proverb that says, "No tree has branches so foolish as to fight among themselves." Many of us in today's world would do well to appreciate that lesson.

Giving to others is more than a mere act of charity. It is something that enhances the very world we live in. When you give to others, you start off something called a "ripple effect." Your generosity spreads out and inspires others to give as well. Giving also helps to keep your character in good form. After all, you can't become a self-centered miser if you practice being generous. You must put at least some of your focus on other people and how the choices you make can affect lives. So when you practice being generous, you help others, yourself and the world at large.

But being generous doesn't necessarily have anything to do with giving away money. You can give people your time, compassion or kind words. You could make an effort to help someone feel appreciated. Many people would consider these gifts to be far more valuable than material goods. In fact, some of the greatest givers in history had little or no money at all. Yet they were able to change the world by using what they had to help others find their own greatness.

Giving back is an unavoidable step on the road to success. There is a difference between being an expert at something and a master. An expert, in any field, has a deep understanding of the techniques and principles of her craft. But a master is one who can also impart that understanding to others. So when you learn something that enhances your life, it is your personal duty to empower others with the same tools.

Many people feel like they will somehow lose something by giving to others. Nothing could be further from the truth. True, you don't want to be a willing victim and allow people to take advantage of you. However, there are several ways that giving can actually increase your ability to receive.

For starters, being generous sends a message to your brain that you have more than enough to go around. If you have the ability to share with others, it must mean that you have plenty of resources yourself. Believing this to be true, the brain then works to find ways of proving it. Your Reticular Activating System jumps into action, drawing to you the people and circumstances you need to live in true abundance.

Secondly, the generosity mindset puts you in a very positive state. It feels really good to help others, to know you've changed someone's life for the better. This is a big part of what the success quotient is all about. See, being generous gives you good feelings, and you already know that we're drawn towards good feelings. Alternatively, when you feel financially, spiritually or emotionally impoverished, you don't have the strength to help anyone else. The feelings that we get from sharing, however, actually inspire us to do better.

Giving back is a great way to put your own positive self-fulfilling prophecy into place. When you produce more for yourself, you can help more people, which in turn makes you feel good, which allows you to produce even more, etc. This is a great cycle, one you definitely want to get into. Remember the whole thing about emotion and experience working together. They create positive mental patterns just as easily as destructive ones. Giving back to others provides you with an internal drive to remain in an influential position. You are compelled to keep doing those things that help you succeed.

Contributing to the greater good also teaches you to have respect for others. In order to give from the heart, you must drop the preconceived notions and prejudices that you may have had about those you help. You must actually think about what things are like from another person's point of view. Other people's difficulties become your difficulties; their suffering becomes your own. Giving appropriate counsel to others can also help you learn more. Teaching people is a great way to reinforce your personal resolve and clarify your own thought process. It also inspires you to hold your own behavior to a higher standard. These are just some of the ways that giving contributes to your overall well-being.

When you give, you are also apt to receive. Have you ever known someone who was just a kind, generous and open-hearted person? Don't you feel compelled to help this person through hard times, to return the consideration and be attentive to his or her needs? Many people talk about being kind and goodhearted, but their actions just don't seem to measure up. People will often forget what you say, but will always remember the way you made them feel. When you show genuine compassion and understanding—when you help others feel good—they will then do whatever it takes to keep that relationship strong. Of course your actions must also be genuine. Don't give just to receive, because that's a focus on self, not others. You need to actually care about people and treat them as you would members of your own family. After all, every one of us is human. We are, in fact, all members of the same family.

You can also give back by donating time, energy or resources to your community. Doing this will give you a sense that you're involved with making a positive impact on the world around you. Community service helps you become a part of something larger than yourself. There are a number of ways that you can help your community grow. You can volunteer to be a "Big Brother" or "Big Sister" and help some young person learn the value of companionship. You can find places to plant trees and flowers for future generations to enjoy. You can donate your time to the homeless shelter or outreach program. Anything you do to help will make a huge impact on the world. Even if you don't see the effects of your work right now, they will emerge through time as what you do ripples out around you.

What you do to others, you do to yourself. What you send out comes right back to you, just like a boomerang. It may not return in the same form or from the same person. But you will eventually get what's coming to you, good or bad. Heed these words and you'll be on your way to making great positive changes in your life.

CHAPTER XVIII:

WORKSHEET

Why is the "me" versus "you" mentality so destructive?

What do you suppose are some of the dangers of becoming greedy?

What are some of ways you can contribute to the lives of other people without giving away money?

What are some ways in which what you send out may come back to you?

What are some areas of your community that you believe need improvement?

What things will you do this month to contribute to those causes?

List at least one person that you can help manage a difficult emotional situation by listening, giving counsel, showing compassion or projecting an attitude of empathy.

What will you do this week to help that person feel better?

Explain your understanding of a "ripple effect."

What is a key difference between an "expert" and a "master?"

When you give to others, what does doing so tell your brain?

What kind of attitude should you have when giving?

How will you start looking at circumstances differently to develop this mentality?

When you talk to people, what will they typically forget and what will they likely remember?

How does giving to your community affect you emotionally?

PART V: YOUR NEW LIFE

CHAPTER XIX

Out With the Old, In With the New

Now, you've set the wheels in motion. You have a powerful plan for achieving your goals and are taking the action steps that will make it happen. But there's something important that you should consider when it comes to improving the quality of your life.

As we agreed earlier, who you are right now is simply a result of your past experiences, understandings and interpretations. As you move toward your goals, however, you'll gain knowledge, develop new routines and learn to perceive things differently. Because of this, you will find yourself becoming wiser and more capable of performing certain tasks. You will develop a more complete understanding of yourself and your surroundings. But this wonderful transformation cannot take place unless you are willing to do away with old belief systems and patterns of behavior. In short, the old you must die as the new you comes to life. This is a concept that throws many people off because it seems at first as though I'm suggesting you should not be yourself. That is definitely not the intention of my message, though. Getting rid of the old you doesn't mean changing your core personality. It simply means that you're expanding yourself, growing and becoming even better. Change is good as long as it represents improvement. One of the worst things that a person can do is try to get better at something while refusing to let go of past limitations. But this is the very thing that stops many people from achieving greatness.

You may want to become better organized, but you will not do so until you decide to let go of your typical time-wasting activities. If you want to develop better relationships, then you can't hold on to the same old communication strategies. It's easy to believe that the way you've handled things until now defines who you are, but that idea is exactly what keeps many people from achieving success.

You may have done certain things in the past, over and over again, but those things don't say anything at all about who you really are. What you did is not who you are—remember that. You've probably made lots of mistakes in the past, but if you believe that those mistakes comprise your identity, you'll never get anywhere in life. When you were child, you thought as a child, but now, you have matured. You have lots of new experiences that flesh out your current version of reality. Learn to view your pathway to success as sort of a "growing up" process. You wouldn't refuse to become an adult simply because you didn't want to let go of childhood opinions. Likewise, accomplishing more will require you to go through a process of intellectual and emotional maturation.

You are not the person who sits in front of the TV for six hours a day. You're not someone who doesn't have any focus or drive. Those are just your old habits, nothing more. You're not shy, reserved, unassertive or anything like that. Again, those are just patterns of behavior. They don't have anything to do with you as a person. In fact, you'll change many times while pursuing your goals, and as long as the change is a move forward, you'll be going in the right direction.

The ways in which you've managed your circumstances until now have placed you exactly where you are at the moment. You can't think that becoming better equipped at managing life somehow diminishes you as a person. You must be prepared to give up your old way of life for a chance at increased pleasure and fulfillment.

And what's so good about the old way of doing things anyway? If you were perfectly happy with the way things were in the past, you wouldn't be seeking improvement and change. We often resist change because of fear—fear of things that are uncertain and unknown—but in order to become better at anything, you must enter an area of performance that you have not yet experienced. Progress, by definition, means that you're doing something you have not done before. This is what makes the fear of change a ridiculous concept.

Don't become addicted to who you were in the past. You wouldn't ride your bicycle in the middle of the street simply because you did so as a child. Since then, you've learned important distinctions about danger and taking risk. That doesn't mean that you've changed who you are. You still have your own unique personality and disposition. Now, you're simply acting with more intelligence because you know a lot more about the same situation. Likewise, it does you no good to reject your own personal development. Perhaps you've never been a big reader of books, but you have recently discovered a reason for doing more with your life. Therefore, it would make no sense to avoid reading the stories of people who have accomplished what you want to achieve. In fact, the process of achievement is the process of "becoming"—becoming someone who's financially intelligent, a better communicator, or more athletic. An important scientific principle holds that two things cannot be in the same place at the same time. This is especially true when it comes to the quality of your life. It makes no sense at all to cling to old patterns of behavior that don't serve you. The process of growth is a process of change. What you have produced up until now is only the result of who you have allowed yourself to become, and it's likely that who you think you are is only an accumulation of ideas taken from family, peers and authority figures. But, your ambitions require that you break out of old conditioning and enter a different experience of life. You cannot remain entirely who you used to be. As it's often said, "Out with the old, and in with the new."

CHAPTER XIX:

WORKSHEET

How can core beliefs about your identity create resistance to change?

Think of some positive changes that you have been reluctant to make simply because you'd feel uncomfortable giving up your old way of doing things. Write them down here.

How has your life been affected by this hesitation to make the appropriate changes?

What is it that you have been afraid of giving up?

What feelings do you receive from whatever was mentioned in the previous answer?

How easy is it for you to feel this way when you know that you're not fulfilling your true potential?

What are some automatic thoughts that might be holding you back from achieving your goals?

In what ways could achieving your goals help you to have more of the desired feelings mentioned earlier?

Have you become generally happier or more discontent by holding yourself back?

If you don't change, what will your life be like in one year from now?

Five years from now?

In ten years?

How would committing to making this change now improve your ability to get more of the emotional states that you want?

CHAPTER XX

What's Next?

It's important that you always keep moving towards a goal. You don't want to achieve what you want and be left asking the question, "Is that all there is?" What makes us feel good is to know that we're moving toward something worthwhile, that we're making progress. That's why I've said before that the journey is often more important than the destination.

Think of your life as a vehicle designed to take you through different experiences in the world. This vehicle is a beautiful, magnificent machine; it's made to improve in performance and serve you better as time goes on. But it doesn't tell you where to go. It simply follows your directions. The question is, "What are you to do with this vehicle?" Are you going to use it to experience the wonderful and amazing world around you? Or would you simply set it to the side and let it rust once you've reached a single destination? It would do you no good to have a new car that simply sat in your driveway year after year. You also wouldn't take it to just one location and then abandon it. You would likely use it for as long as you could to take you wherever you needed to go.

So, as you move toward your current goal, get an idea of where you'd like your next stop to be—or shall I say your next beginning?

Achieving what you want right now, after all, will not be the conclusion of your journey. There will be plenty of other roads to travel, boundaries to cross and challenges to face. Think of what I said before about the world being in a constant state of evolution. The person who doesn't continue to grow will soon fall far behind.

Many businesses no longer exist, even though they were highly profitable in the past. As times change, a company that wants to remain successful must improve and alter its approach. Otherwise, its success will simply be a passing trend, a fad that cannot be sustained.

You are, in fact, your own company. You are the CEO, president and director. As in any corporation, the skills you acquire today may soon be rendered obsolete. It is your job to continue moving forward. You must continue to develop yourself and grow. If not, your success will also come and go just as easily.

Many times in your life you may have seen a homeless person sitting on a street corner, in front of a store or under a tree drinking alcohol. We can have a tendency to look at some of these people, from time to time, and become a little judgmental. After all, it seems as though they're just wasting their lives, scraping up just enough money each day to satisfy their addictions. But if you were to actually stop and talk to some of those people, you'll discover that each has a very different story and background.

Many of them were doing well in life at one time or another. They might have even accomplished a certain measure of success. Some of the people you see on the street once had a house and car, and perhaps a family. But they didn't plan to keep up with life. Challenges arose that they were not prepared to manage. Times changed and they didn't.

When the lives they created started to crumble, it became so painful that all they wanted to do was avoid what was happening. Soon, they found that alcohol or some other mind-altering substance could numb the pain very quickly, and it became much easier to avoid dealing with problems by becoming intoxicated than by developing the strength to deal with them.

See, when you assume that what you have is all there is, you become attached to everything staying the same. If you think that way, and something happens to your so-called perfect life, the change will send you into a psychological tailspin.

Many people face similar challenges and don't take the road into substance abuse. Some people are more prepared to roll with the changes and choose not to run away from them. Let's take, for example, Donald Trump, whose example I discussed earlier. Remember, he isn't the only wealthy person who ever lost a lot of money. Lots of people in similar positions suffered financial collapse. But some of those people ended up committing suicide or becoming that person sitting in front of the liquor store.

So how did Donald Trump get through his difficulties and become even better at what he does the second time around? I'll let "The Donald," as he's commonly called, answer that one himself. Trump once said, "Sometimes, by losing a battle, you find a new way to win the war." You need to be prepared to take things to the next level, to seek out a new frontier. Growth is what it's all about.

Once you reach your financial goals, it's going to take some work to stay there and continue finding fulfillment. You may have to figure out how you can add more value to your chosen industry. You could learn ways to create residual income streams that will pay your family for generations to come. You may want to increase your contribution efforts and help other people achieve their goals. You may simply set a bigger financial goal. The important thing is that you keep moving.

Say you marry the woman or man of your dreams. Now, find out how you can make that relationship as good and strong as possible. You could plan to go around the world together, or perhaps settle down and have kids. You may want to build a family centered on communication, honesty and mutual respect. Or perhaps you may work at discovering how you and your mate can become the best of friends. How many marriages fail because two people get together and stop growing with each other right then? They reach the goal of getting married—they've won the prize—and have no further motivation to stay involved.

A relationship is a living, breathing organism. It has to be nurtured and cared for. If a relationship is not growing, then it's dying. Two people who were once madly in love can easily find themselves drifting apart.

What about your personal development goals? If you want to be a public speaker, then you have to always have fresh new ideas and concepts. People will get tired of hearing the same old stories and learning concepts that they already know. You have to continue improving whatever you do in some way.

Some people say, "I've set my goal and when I reach it, I will have hit my mark." The truth is that there is no mark. There is no finish line. You're on a voyage that started the minute you were born and will not end until you take your last breath. Remember that some people physically die when they have nothing left to look forward to. Don't get caught in that trap.

Your goals will change as you grow and mature. Therefore, you must continue to create new challenges for yourself, to always give yourself something to reach for.

Remember the previous chapter about raising the bar and bettering your best. When you finally find that you can jump high enough to reach a certain goal, you want to raise your target and go after something more challenging. Remember that human beings are goal-oriented creatures. We feel best when we're making progress and moving toward something that has value. As Reverend Robert Schuller, an American minister, once said, "Success is never ending."

It's good to be content with what you have, but never be satisfied with where you are. There's always more to do, more to give, more to create, and you deserve to give your very best while on this short trip called life. For all relative purposes, human potential is virtually unlimited. How high can you go? How much good can you bring into the world? Nobody knows—not even you. Therefore, it is your duty to keep giving your best every single day that you wake up. If you're still here, that means that you have more to do. You'll never, ever create your very best. There will always be a new mountain to climb.

This is not saying that you should work yourself to the bone, but the human mind needs to stay active. Your brain is somewhat like a muscle in the sense that if you don't use it, you lose it. You'll never get to a point where you no longer need to interact with life.

Many people in our society are under the misconception that once you've made it, it's time to sit back and rest on your accomplishments. But look at the most successful people in any field. They are constantly producing, creating, getting better and offering more value to others. That's what keeps them on top. A life that is not going anywhere is boring and lacks fulfillment.

If you were to buy a new house, wouldn't you want to decorate it, beautify it and make it even better than it was when you moved in? Think of what would happen if you moved into the same house and did nothing to it. Grass would be growing wild and out of control. The interior would be covered with dust and debris. The floors and carpets would be filled with dirt tracked in from outside. The entire place would be a wreck in almost no time at all. A house must be maintained in order for it to remain comfortable and pleasing to the eye. But the people who reside there must actually make improvements to the property if they wish to continue enjoying it. We all know this fact, but many people don't choose to view their lives in the same way. Following your dreams is like building a structure. Your mindset is the blueprint, preparation is the foundation and action is the process of laying down one brick at a time. Once your house is fully constructed, what will you do with it? Will you update the landscaping and slap a fresh coat of paint on it every other year? Would you like to add on an additional room in the future—or maybe two or three? Are you going to make both the inside and outside of this creation immaculate, or will you simply let it sit and fall prey to the elements? How would beautifying your current level of achievement help you to feel better about yourself and your potential?

See, how you feel controls what you will do. Many people confuse this principle. They believe that what they think determines how they will act. But have you ever started out a day knowing that you need to complete a certain task and put it off simply because you weren't properly motivated? All of us neglect to do certain things that we know are good for us. If thought were the only thing needed to create action, then most of us would be far more productive than we are. Now, if you keep your mind on a particular undertaking, concentrate on it and imagine how good the end result would make you feel, then you'd probably get motivated enough to act. But it's the potential of positive emotions that actually inspire you to do something, and until you feel like doing something, you simply won't take action. You may say, "Then how does someone who hates her job continue going to work day after day?" In this case, the person is still motivated by emotions. The pleasure of having the things that money can buy, like food, electricity and shelter, could be more motivating than the difficulty of going to work. Or, this person may feel that not going to work will cause her to lose those things that she truly enjoys. If this person did not like the job and had no feelings motivating her to go, however, she would simply quit.

Even someone who stays in an abusive relationship may have an emotional incentive to do so. Perhaps she was brought up to believe that you should never leave your mate and therefore she associates separation with a great deal of pain. She could have a terrible fear of abandonment and through the years that fear has become more painful than the process of being abused.

This is why it's important to identify your dominating emotions. The feelings that drive you are so important because the way you feel about things can either help you succeed or cause you to fail.

As you come closer to your goals, you should have an idea of where you want to take yourself next. But don't get in the habit of looking too far ahead too quickly. Doing this can actually slow your progress. True, you want to have an end goal in mind, and you want that goal to be big, so that it motivates you to go beyond your comfort zone. However, you can't look past important steps that are needed to bring you to the next point of your success.

Let's say that you're going to run a 100-mile race. Each mile is marked by a waving flag posted on a tall pole. So, you begin to run and start making your way towards the finish line. You steadily pass the first, second and third mile markers. At this point, it would do you no good to focus only on the 97 miles left to go. Doing that would probably make you feel completely overwhelmed and hinder your ability to continue the race. All you need to concern yourself with is making it to the next pole. Once you get there, you will be able to see the next milestone ahead, and when you get to that point, the next target will become visible and so on.

This is the same way you run the path of ever-increasing success. Once you reach your initial goal, you'll be able to see the next one just ahead, and when you get to that point, the next objective will make itself clear. You don't have to think of doing everything at one time. In fact, it would be very unreasonable to do so. All you have to do is make it to that next spot, and you'll find that the pathway ahead continues to open up new and exciting opportunities.

When you go through life in this way, your days would be filled with passion. You don't need an alarm clock to wake you up in the morning because you can't wait to just get out there and see what happens next. People who are great in any field don't have to push themselves out the door. They know that something new and wonderful is waiting just around the corner and they are committed to making the most out of every single day.

What you do is often less important than how you do it. You can go to your job every day and never rise above the ceiling of mediocrity. Your time would be better spent thinking about exactly how you are doing your job and how you approach clients, coworkers and superiors. The average person spends all day watching the clock and does just enough to get by, but you have separated yourself from the pack. You've decided to go that extra mile—to do more than what you're expected to do and create powerful bonds with those you encounter every day. This is entirely your choice. You can either live your life with an enormous amount of passion or just go through the motions hoping to get by.

Remember, you're trying to break habitual routines that don't get you anywhere. It would make no sense to simply substitute one stale routine for another. In my sales training classes, I always tell my students that a great salesperson learns how to look at each prospect as an individual. That way, every day is fresh and exciting. Each appointment is filled with new challenges and possibilities. You, too, can create this kind of excitement in your everyday life. The key is to keep moving forward, to find new ways of getting even more out of whatever you do. The fact that you're here on this earth means you have the wonderful opportunity to experience life in a way that no one else has before. You are a creator, an individual expression of the unlimited universal energy that connects us all. For this reason, it is imperative that you use your powers of imagination and concentration to continuously bring new things into existence.

CHAPTER XX:

WORKSHEET

Once you've achieved your current goals, in what ways could you recommit to a new level of success?

How can you improve your performance in any activity that you're really good at now?

How can you create new challenges for yourself in your current line of work? For example, you might make 25 sales calls instead of 15, or you might cut your waste costs by 10 percent.

How much would you enjoy overcoming some of your greatest challenges?

Why can it hurt you to "take it easy" once you've achieved your initial goal?

How can you add some "flash" to your normal, everyday routines?

What are some of the things you have done that have allowed you to achieve certain degrees of success in different areas of your life?

Have you stopped performing some of these activities now that you've reached a certain measure of accomplishment?

How will you now start to revisit these former rituals in a way that adds value to what you already do?

CHAPTER XXI

Pain and Pleasure

Earlier, we discussed how pain and pleasure are key motivating factors in your life. In this chapter, we're going to specifically break down these concepts on a deeper level. Understanding pain and pleasure is so important if you want to get into the business of mastering your life.

Think about a simple action, like walking to the store. Why would you want to walk to the store? Well, the most obvious answer is that you wish to buy something there. Let's say that you want to get some ice cream and the pleasure of eating it outweighs the work involved in walking. Or, maybe you have a headache and you're going to the store for some pain reliever. In that case, the chance to avoid your physical pain is what motivates you to go. On the other hand, you may not really need anything. You might just want to take a relaxing walk outside. Again, that's the power of pleasure at work. Perhaps your home is chaotic and you just want to get away. Then, you may be motivated both to avoid the pain in your home and receive pleasure from going out for a calm, peaceful walk.

There are four things to look at in any situation that you want to change. We are going to explore each one of these individually. I want to express these four elements of motivation in question form, and I invite you to pose these questions to yourself.

1.   What pleasure do you get from staying where you are?

2.   What pleasure would you receive from moving into a new way of life?

3.   What is it about staying in your current conditions that causes you pain?

4.   What pain would you receive from moving into a new way of life?

If you want to do something like change jobs, but don't find yourself taking action, ask yourself these four questions. First, ask yourself what pleasure you receive from staying at your current position. Your answers may include things like: security, the comfort of knowing your job, familiarity, and workplace friendships. Now, move on to the second question. What pleasure would you receive from getting the job that you want? You may say a larger income, more freedom to make decisions, more responsibility or a platform to put your ideas in motion. Next, go to the third question. What is painful about remaining where you are now? Maybe you've simply outgrown your current position and find yourself going through the motions, day after day. You may be unfulfilled and feel you are not being given due respect by supervisors. Perhaps you are working longer hours for less pay and know that you can do more. Next, go to the fourth question. What is painful about moving into a new way of life? Maybe your mind perceives a certain loss in changing. Maybe the risk involved in changing jobs is scary or you worry about not fitting into a new work culture.

Look at an area of your life that you'd like to change and ask yourself these four questions. Take out a piece of paper and, with a pencil or pen, section it into four equal parts. At the top of each section, write a phrase that represents one of these four questions. Over column one, write "Pleasure of Staying." At the top of column two, put "Pleasure of Leaving." Three is "The Pain of Staying" and four is "The Pain of Leaving." Then, think about your current dilemma and fill each section in accordingly. Afterwards, you can look at what you've written objectively and come to an educated decision.

Asking yourself these questions will help you clarify your position and decide the importance of making your next move. So, we'll assume you've already discovered that you'll get much more pleasure from moving to a new job than you are currently receiving. When you look at your list, you may also find that there are way more items in the "Pain of Staying" category and only a handful in the "Pain of Leaving." In that case, the decision about what you should do is pretty clear.

Let's assume that the pleasure of staying in your current position outweighs the potential pleasure of moving forward. You should then take a look at the pain categories. How does the pain of leaving measure up against the pain of staying? I'm not here to tell you which decision is right or wrong. That is entirely up to you. But when you analyze things in this way, it gives you a great deal of power in deciding what you truly want to do.

You have to take both the pleasure and pain sides into consideration when going through this process. But you must also ask yourself, "What is most important to me?" You may be lined up to endure ten painful things once you make the decision to change, but the joy of achieving your goals may exceed all of those things combined. Conversely, you may have a number of items in your pleasure of changing category, but even all of those things may not be worth the sacrifice. You may be an artist of some sort and desire to book an engagement for every day of the year. But practicing, performing and building your skill-set may leave no time to enjoy family, friends and life in general.

Performing this exercise helps you put things into perspective. It also allows you to determine whether your efforts and priorities are in line. You may not really want exactly what you believe that you do. You may not be completely satisfied with what you have right now. You need to know where you stand and how each of your goals measures up to your ideal life.

You can also make the "Pain and Pleasure" principle *work* for you. How do you get something that you really, really want? How can you motivate yourself to do the difficult things that will get you to your goal? The answer is simple. Associate an enormous amount of pleasure with having what you want and an equal amount of pain with not getting it. Connect an incredible sense of pleasure to doing those things that help you improve and just as much or more pain to avoiding them. This is a simple yet powerful way to live with purpose.

I'm going to give you an example of how to do this. Let's say that you want to improve your physical health. You have the outcome clearly in mind, have prepared well, but just don't seem motivated enough to take action. Now I'm going to show you how to ignite your inner sense of passion by using the abovementioned exercise.

First, you'll want to make out your pleasure and pain list. Remember the four categories we discussed earlier that relate to where you are in life right now. Now, because you want to be motivated, we're going to use these results in a very specific way.

Look at the second column of your list, the one that states the pleasure you will receive from getting in better shape. You have things like: more energy, better posture, more flexibility and a longer, more fulfilled life. Now, focus on these results. Really imagine yourself having that ideal body right now. Create a mental picture of how you will look like when you've achieved your goal. Step into that image, so that it is you. Make the colors brighter. Feel what it's like to be healthy; feel that energy and emotional boost. Notice how strong you feel now. Really get a sense of the power you possess. Feel yourself standing taller, walking with more grace and fluidity. Notice how you breathe when you feel like this. Think of what others will say when they see you. Go through a typical day, imagining yourself doing fun activities and feeling absolutely wonderful. Imagine wearing that perfect outfit—you know, the one that would really make your new body shine. Imagine looking in the mirror and seeing yourself being thinner, more fit and full of life. Notice how natural it feels to just smile, because you look fantastic. You sleep comfortably each night and feel fully rested. You have more than enough energy to do everything you want to do during the day. The key is to really get into this. Get into the most powerful state that you can as you think about everything you'll receive from being fit. Now store this image in your head as "The New Me" image.

Now, look at the third category on your list. This one describes the pain of staying at your current fitness level. You might have put things down like: low energy, bad mood, overweight, loss of breath and clothes don't fit. Now, really consider how these things have been burdening you. In fact, think of how your life will be in the future if you don't change. Imagine yourself becoming even more overweight and out of shape than you are now. Make a mental picture of how you will look and step into that body once again. Really feel the burden of carrying those extra pounds. Notice how weak you are now because you didn't improve your health. You have a lower energy level than you did before. Make the colors of that image darker and duller. Your emotional state is low and you don't feel that good about yourself. Imagine that you're looking in a mirror and see how your body has changed for the worse. Feel how difficult it is taking each breath. You can't do anything for very long without stopping for air. Really feel the pain of staying in your current condition and notice how that pain increases as time goes on. Take yourself even further into the future. By this time you probably developed certain physical disorders. You may have high blood pressure, high cholesterol, diabetes and/or any number of adverse conditions. You have to take numbers of prescriptions just to manage the symptoms of being out of shape. And those medications make you feel like crap. Get all the way into this experience, so that you feel the pain flowing through every cell and fiber of your being. Now store this image in your head as "The Unhealthy Me" image.

What we're doing is giving your mind such a contrast that it naturally moves you toward your desired goal. Your brain at this point will automatically compare "The New Me" image to "The Unhealthy Me" image because it wants to seek pleasure and avoid pain. Taking these two steps alone may be enough to "turn on" your inner drive. But let's take this exercise even further to make the change to really stick. We're going to take the items in the other two categories of your list and "Reframe" them. This means that we are going to look at them from a new perspective to gain new understandings.

So look at the first column. This is your "pleasure of staying the same" section. You may have things written down like: being lazy and comfortable, eating what I want and just enjoying life. But really think about these answers. You know that if you achieve your ideal body, you'll feel stronger, have more energy and be in a better mood. Wouldn't you feel more comfortable in your body—with yourself—if you were fit and shape? Would you enjoy life more if you had a better attitude, more energy and were able to go out and do the things you wanted to? Because how comfortable can you really feel when your clothes don't fit and you're short of breath most of the time? How happy are you when you look at yourself in the mirror and see your body slowly breaking down? Will you really be able to feel comfortable as you deteriorate, get weaker and become prone to injury? It actually takes a lot of work to be out of shape. It's a strain to do the simplest things. You become less capable of performing simple tasks and have to burden others for help. How embarrassing will it be when others must do things for you that you should be able to do yourself? How good would you feel about that? Some people think that it's okay to let their health slip because they're just enjoying life. But physical decline of this sort really involves a lot of suffering. And you can't just eat what you want to when you're in bad shape. Someone with high blood pressure often starts to feel dizzy after eating a few bites of salty food. Diabetics have to avoid consuming all kinds of things, else they go into shock or die. A person who's in good shape, however, can eat rich or sweet foods in moderation without suffering those kinds of negative effects. Really consider whether you truly get pleasure from staying the same, and note your findings.

Now, look at the fourth column, in which you wrote down the pain of changing. There may be things in it like: it will take a lot of work, my body will hurt and it won't feel good. But let's think about these things in a new way. Consider how much work it is to be really out of shape. You can work hard to get worse or work hard to get better. Which would you prefer? Since you're working hard either way, wouldn't it make sense to put that effort towards something that will give you a benefit? Eventually, your body will get stronger and using it to work out will become easier. Plus, you will get all the benefits of being in shape. The work it takes to stay in bad physical condition, on the other hand, is only going to get harder. Plus, you'll receive a lot of negative consequences in return. Now, consider what you listed about the body hurting while getting in shape. Look at this idea from the opposite perspective. Think about how susceptible you are to injury when your bones, muscles and tendons are weak. Being out of shape also means that your body heals more slowly. So the pain you suffer will continue much longer. Your immune system will also have weakened, so you'll likely contract illnesses several times each year. And how painful is that? How much work does it take to get through the flu and other crippling illnesses every few months? You probably can't sleep too well, because your body just can't get comfortable at night and being overweight makes it harder to breathe. Take some time getting into this experience, the same way that you did with the other three, and note your findings.

Now, you have used the pain and pleasure principle in a way that dramatically increases your likelihood of achieving success. Basically, you have given your brain an offer that it cannot refuse. You have spelled every consequence out so clearly that there really is no other reasonable option but to achieve your goal. Every part of the equation has been framed in a way that moves you toward your desired outcome. Whenever your brain looks to review the pain and pleasure of getting in shape, it will come up with the same answer. No matter which way you look at the issue—you win! Isn't that splendid? Doing this exercise really stacks the deck in your favor, but you need to really involve yourself in the process by involving all of your five senses, and make sure that you're fully engaged in imagining the different outcomes and changes that will happen in your life. Condition yourself to consistently do this, and you will discover more drive, commitment and passion towards achieving your goals than you ever thought possible.

CHAPTER XXI:

WORKSHEET

Write down an activity that you made a conscious decision to do recently. You can pick something simple, as in our "walking to the store" example.

What are the four questions you will use to examine your motivations for change?

Consider a situation that you desire to improve. In this area, what is the:
Pleasure of staying where you are?

Pleasure of achieving something new?

Pain of staying where you are?

Pain of achieving something new?

Look at the second category. Imagine yourself having all of these things. How will your life be different?

What will you be ready to accomplish once you have achieved these things?

How will your mindset, attitude and outlook towards life change?

What difference will that make for you?

Look at the third category now. How have these issues burdened you until now?

What will your life look like in five years, if you don't make this change?

10 years?

20 years?

Take a look at the first category. How can achieving what you want actually help you to have even more of these things?

Move on to the last category. How does staying where you are cause you to experience many of these issues now?

How will it get worse, over time, if you don't make the change?

Which of your fourth category items will actually subside and empower you, once you've pushed through the initial pain?

How has doing this exercise changed your perspective?

CHAPTER XXII

The Importance of Progress

In this book, you've read many times about the value of moving forward in life. But, at this point, I think it's vital to specifically talk about the importance of progress. We all need food and water and sleep to give us a physical life. Progress, however, is what gives us an emotional and psychological life. Human beings are made to develop and grow. These things are a part of our natural heritage. We have an instinctive need to improve and advance. This is part of what separates mankind from the animals. A cat can't be anything but a cat. It doesn't have the capacity or intention to go beyond its inborn nature. You and I, however, have infinite potential. We are designed to get better and better with time.

Lots of people start an exercise program and then quit before they ever reach their fitness goals. But what inspires that person who continues to work out and train until he reaches his desired weight? It's progress—getting rid of those first few pounds or seeing that first ripple of muscle starting to show. Progress opens up a world of possibilities and inspires you to imagine what else may be possible.

Of course in order to achieve anything new, you have to be committed to making progress. You may have heard the saying "Insanity is doing the same things over and over again and expecting different results." Yet many people do just that when it comes to going after a goal. The only way to know that you're moving toward is by checking your results and seeing if they're improving over time.

Improvement is what keeps you going. When a person sets out to get rid of fifty pounds, he doesn't expect to do it all at once. Thinking that way would be a quick road to discouragement and failure. But when he sees those small changes taking place—that belt-line steadily shrinking, his muscles becoming more toned—he really gets fired up to keep going.

Seeing improvement is what drives us to achieve even better results. So don't focus on being perfect, just make progress. If you do this, those little wins will soon add up to an enormous positive change.

See, the problem is that too many people focus on being perfect right at the start of any undertaking. You may look at someone who's a great producer in a certain area and try to do things just like him. Of course, you're going to fall very short of that goal at first. After failing to meet that perfect ideal just a handful of times, most people give up. To them, it seems like doing what they really want is an impossible task. But no one starts doing anything perfectly. Even the person you really admire was probably extremely unskilled and incompetent at one time. We often think that people who are really good at something were just born doing it well. It seems as though they have some sort of genetic tendency to perform that other people don't posses. These ideas, however, are nothing but myths. It's true that some people are simply gifted in a particular area, but such exceptional inborn talent is almost too rare to consider.

Successful people are where they are because they've practiced doing things over time that eventually lead to success. They've allowed themselves to make mistakes along the way, but they continued moving forward with passion and determination. Eventually, they reached the elite level of performance that you see today. That is why it seems like doing certain things are so easy for some people. They have gone through the hard times and have come out on the other side. There's a saying that goes, "Anything worth doing, is worth doing well." I'd like to switch that phrase around a bit and say, "Anything worth doing is worth doing badly." You must be willing to not be good at something and keep doing it anyway, over and over again, until you develop the skills and competency to perform well.

You'll have to go through periods of feeling awkward and confused; times when it seems like you have no idea what you're doing. Most people are terribly afraid of such emotional states and will do almost anything to avoid them. But, if you make yourself endure the initial difficulties, you will start building skill. The feelings you'll get by increasing your abilities will be more than worth the trouble. You'll soon start to notice yourself making those little steps of progress that we talked about earlier. That will make you feel much more motivated to pursue your ultimate goal. You'll also get better at the task, which means that the results you produce next time are likely to be even better. This will set up a pattern that helps you feel good every step of the way. It works whether you're talking about improving your career, family life, relationships or anything else you pursue.

Making progress is also essential to our survival. Let me give you an example of what I mean. In the 1980s, virtually all commercial music was put onto magnetic tape and sold as an audio cassette. As time went on, compact disc technology became available to the public and slowly edged out audio tapes. Now, most music is put into digital format and sold via the Internet.

Let me ask you a question: How well do you think an audio cassette-player store would do in today's market? I suppose you've guessed that the answer is "Not very well." Sure there may be a few people who'd buy such a machine for the sake of nostalgia. But, it's more than likely that this type of business would soon go bankrupt. Music store owners had to adjust if they wanted to stay relevant through changing times. Most have now put up websites where you can go and download songs in an instant. Advances in technology required music companies to progress, to change the way they did business.

You know that a loaf of bread costs much more than it did just ten years ago. You may make a thousand dollars a week today and find that income adequate to supply your needs. In the future, however, that same amount of money might not be sufficient. So you have to get better just to maintain what you already have. Let's go beyond that idea, because you want to flourish and not simply make ends meet. If you want to have a life of freedom and fulfillment, then you'll need to get in the habit of making progress.

Happy feelings come from being fully engaged in life. They arrive as a result of approaching daily circumstances in a spirit of creativity and playfulness. The happiest people you know are probably very curious about the world. They are always expecting to find something really cool around the next corner. With this kind of attitude, life is like an adventure. You never know exactly what's going to happen next, but you're really interested in finding out. Too often, we treat life like something we're afraid of. We just try to stay out of the way, hoping not to get noticed. Somehow, many of us are fooled into believing that once we've reached a certain position, our jobs are done.

As renowned motivational speaker Les Brown once said, "You can't get out of life alive." It does no good to accomplish something, and then try to find a position where you can take cover. There's no value in being a spectator. You may as well step up to the plate and start swinging at a few more balls. You might be right on the verge of making a world record hit. No place in life is completely safe. You'll never get to a place where it's okay to stand on the sidelines and watch others take action. It's okay to celebrate your accomplishments. Enjoy your money, your success, and the fruits of your labor, but know that you're not trying to get someplace where you can just sit down and stay there. In order to have a life full of fun and freedom, it's important to continue to grow and develop yourself. What you experience in life is really just a projection of your inner world. When your inner world is in decline, your circumstances will soon reflect it.

CHAPTER XXII:

WORKSHEET

What is the primary goal that you are dedicating yourself to achieving right now?

Once you have accomplished that goal, in what ways can you get even more fulfillment out of that area of your life?

In what ways could continual progress prove essential to your survival?

How does continuing to develop and grow help you become more satisfied with life?

What are some goals that you have recently achieved or are about to fulfill?

How will you "Raise the Bar" in these areas, so that you have something else to stretch for?

How does the myth of natural ability keep people from going through what it takes to succeed?

List some areas where this misconception might have held you back in the past.

What things in your life are worth doing badly until you can do them well?

How does acting in a spirit of curiosity keep you engaged with life?

List some action steps that you will take and persist with until you develop the skill to make progress.

CHAPTER XXIII

Measure Your Progress

If you want to continue to move forward in life, you have to be able to tell when you're on course. Your success has to be measureable. Otherwise, how will you know when you have it? One of the key differences between those who get what they want out of life and those who don't is the practice of measuring results.

Progress is the act of taking steps forward, of doing something better than you've done so far. In order to achieve it, you have to know both where you've been and where you're at. That way you can make sure that you're making progress and not sliding backwards.

For you to get anywhere in life, you have to be honest about where you are at any moment. As I've said before, some people find this to be a very difficult thing to do, mostly because they feel a sense of shame about not being where they want to be. They get defensive and rationalize that things are going better than they actually are. This type of response comes from the ego. The ego is a false persona. It is a projection of the person you would like others to believe you are. Your ego is a mask that covers the parts of your personality you are ashamed of. It tries to keep you from psychological harm by hiding your own flaws, weaknesses and incongruities from yourself and others. But doing this will not help you succeed. In order to achieve greatness, you must develop the ability to be brutally honest with yourself. This will likely be very uncomfortable at first, and doing it well will take practice. What you're trying to do is get to the point where you can look at your own behaviors and emotions as a casual observer. Once you can do this, you'll be able to measure your progress accurately. Remember that we're driven by emotions, those things that happen beneath the surface. The stories you've become accustomed to telling yourself about your behavior may not be completely truthful.

Next, you have to determine where you want to be. We've already covered some of this in earlier chapters, but it's especially important to go over this process again. You need to get clear about where it is that you really want to see yourself at the end. Once you know where you are and where you want to be, you can set a series of benchmarks between those two points. Make it so that each successive step is a move up from the previous position. Every milestone that you achieve should represent a new level of growth. And since you have a detailed description of where you are right now, you also know what's better than that. This is important because you have to know when you're creating an actual positive change and when you're simply spinning your wheels.

Let's say that you want to write a book like this one. Obviously, you can break that book into different sections, separate those sections into chapters and further divide those chapters into paragraphs, sentences and words. But you have to constitute what progress means for you. If you only write a couple of paragraphs every week, it might take years to finish your manuscript. In addition, you will need time to be creative and organize ideas in a way that flows smoothly for the reader. So how do you figure it all out?

In any task, like writing, you can refine both your process and approach. What if your mind is really scattered, and you find it hard to think clearly? Perhaps you should create a detailed outline for your book before writing. You could take notes on where you want it to go from start to finish, and then add in all the important points and subcategories. This would make a big improvement in your thought process when it comes to writing. The act of simply creating an outline, therefore, is a progressive step. It is something you can do that helps you achieve your goal even more efficiently. What if you want to get better organized with your workload? You'd first need to find out exactly how you're spending your time on a daily basis. Take a couple of days to write down everything you do during the course of a 24-hour period. Document both your productive and unproductive behaviors. Don't leave anything out. Then you can step back, look at what you're doing and develop a clear strategy for making progress. You might find out that you spend way too much time each day sorting through nonessential emails. Perhaps you've been managing too many of other people's responsibilities. But now that you see what's going wrong, you can take steps to improve your performance.

You may want to save those emails for the end of your day. You could practice focusing more on your own duties or simply delegate unimportant tasks. Because you've learned to assess things accurately, you'll know when you're truly making a difference.

I once read about a basketball coach who turned a losing team into champions during the course of one year. He did it by insisting that each athlete improve several parts of his game by only 2%. It was a very simple, yet sophisticated, training strategy. Anybody can improve by 1 or 2 percent in almost anything because it's such a short stretch from what the person has already been doing. But when a player makes this type of progress in several areas it has a significant positive impact on his entire game. When the whole team does this, they can easily improve their ranking in a year's time.

The same is true when it comes to your own life. The beautiful thing about making progress is that any change is a *change*—even if it's only a 2% one. Can you perform 2% better at your job? Of course you can. Could you spend just 2% more time with your children or your spouse? Sure you could. Could you stay up 30 minutes longer or wake up 30 minutes earlier so that you'll have focused time to work on your goals? Absolutely.

We're not talking about enormous adjustments here. The big change will come in time. All you have to do is be just a little better than you were the day, week and month before. But getting a clear picture of both your current and potential circumstances lets you know which way you're heading and how far you've gone until now. The next major step would be to set up your deadlines.

When you're setting goals, it can be good to establish a deadline. Though you don't want to get too attached to having things turn out exactly the way that you've planned, a reasonable deadline can work well as a tool for keeping your efforts on track.

Think about how commercial offers are almost always made "For a limited time." This is because advertisers know that many people will only take action when pressed with a deadline. Many people only get motivated to satisfy an obligation at the last minute. Think of how many students try to cram three weeks of study into the night before an exam. Lots of people don't even think about paying a bill until that "Final Notice" arrives in the mail. It can be very human to put off completing a job until something or someone makes it a priority. But you can also use this tendency to your advantage. Setting a deadline can put you under the pressure you need to take whatever actions are necessary in the moment. The interesting thing is that a deadline should be both within and outside of reason.

In order to achieve what you really want, you must make a point to venture outside your comfort zone. This means setting a goal that is beyond what you would normally expect to accomplish. You don't want to play it safe and only reach for things that are firmly within your grasp. At the same time, however, you must shoot for something that makes you stretch, that takes you beyond the limits of your current understanding. This is why your goals should not be entirely reasonable. Your current position in life reflects what you already deem to be normal, customary and achievable. You must, therefore, begin to somewhat stretch beyond what you previously thought to be possible.

So, you must strategically determine how to measure your results. Your deadlines can be neither too large nor too small, but you must choose a way of setting milestones that are useful to your own personal development. A time frame also makes it easier to reduce large goals into manageable tasks. Once you decide when you want something to happen, you can determine which action steps will make it work. You start making distinctions between where you are and where you want to go. This takes away a lot of the stress of choosing where to begin.

A fifty-pound weight-loss goal can be separated into five-pound increments. You can focus on earning an extra 417 dollars per month, instead of 5,000 dollars a year. You can even break down that goal further into 13 dollars per day. Doesn't it seem much easier to do, once you put your goal into these terms? You can utilize this same process when setting milestones for anything you want to achieve.

Determine a specific number and time frame when considering your monetary goals. If you want to make more social contacts, decide how many new people you will talk to each day. You can gauge your fitness goals according to weight loss, endurance, strength gains or appearance. In any case, you should have a specific set of criteria to evaluate your progress at each step.

CHAPTER XXIII:

WORKSHEET

Pick an area of your life in which it would be useful for you to do better. What, specifically, does that part of your life look like right now?

Exactly how would that part of your life change, if things were ideal?

What developmental milestones fall between your current and optimal conditions? Examples of such milestones might be getting into the habit of following a schedule or developing a more efficient system for sorting mail.

List a few small improvements that could add up to big results in your life.

What productive behaviors do you perform on a daily basis?

What are some of your unproductive habits?

What things could you do better by just 1 or 2 percent to significantly improve the quality of your life?

How has your ego "masked" the need for improvement in certain areas of your life until now?

If you were to be really brutally honest with yourself, what could you be doing better right now?

CHAPTER XXIV

Control Your Language

You have to be conscious about what you say. Your words have the incredible power to both build you up and tear you down. The language you habitually use will largely determine the quality of your experiences.

Language not only describes life but also creates the filters through which you will experience it and the boundaries that limit your experience of it. It's said that Eskimos have over one hundred words to describe the word "snow." Because of the climate they live in, they have to make more distinctions about ice than most people in other parts of the word. Eskimos must know which snow is best to build a structure upon and which is best to create drinking water. They have different words for soft snow, frozen snow and snow that is tainted with seal oil or fur. Because of this, Eskimos experience snow in many more ways than most of us do. While most of us have one or two different ways of thinking about snow, Eskimos have a much more complex and enriched view of the subject. One of the reasons they experiences snow differently from you and me is that they use a language that is built to hold an advanced understanding of icy conditions.

Language plays a key role in your life as well. Think about a time when you may have lost your car keys. You might have looked all around the house—on tables, chairs and countertops—without any luck whatsoever. All the time, you could be saying things in your head like, "I can never find my keys," "Why can't I find my keys," or "I just don't know where my keys are." At these times, it is very likely that someone else in your household will simply walk over to a table that you already looked at, pick up your car keys, and say, "Here they are." Now, you know that you looked on that specific table for the keys. But they were not there. What happened was that you were repeating those words "I can't find my keys" and "I can never find my keys." Your brain took those words as direct instructions. What goes on in these types of scenarios, when you look for an item in a certain area and not see it even though it's there? What happened is that your brain deleted your awareness of the keys because you were commanding it not to find them. This is a very common way that language can affect the outcome of our lives.

Think about how you talk to yourself on a regular basis. Are you in the habit of telling yourself that things just won't work out? Perhaps you continuously recount your past failures and setbacks. You may tell yourself that you're either a night owl or an early morning person. And you know that these words often identify and support whoever it is that you think you are.

When people say, for instance, that they just can't get a good night's sleep, they play that idea out. Don't they? These people repeatedly go without needed rest because being overworked and tired is how they see themselves to be. However, a morning person always rises early to get a jump on the day. He or she feels very comfortable with getting up much earlier than most people. This is because being a morning person has become an identity level concept.

The things that we say to ourselves are often very subtle and quiet. They may simply emerge as feelings or an intuitive sense of how we should act in any moment. You literally talk yourself into things—into believing, feeling and behaving the way you think you ought to. This is why it's very important to be attentive to what comes out of your mouth. We talk to ourselves automatically, without thinking. Your customary reactions often go by so fast that you don't even realize what you may be verbalizing to yourself.

You want to monitor the way you talk to yourself. You need to discover exactly what your internal dialogue, emotions and intuitions are telling you. First, notice what you're feeling at any time. Your feelings are responses to the thoughts you think. When you analyze your feelings, you can determine what the messages are that lie behind them.

So whenever you have a feeling or emotion that disempowers you, ask yourself "Beyond this feeling, what's going on?" What kind of things are you saying to yourself that have worked to produce that feeling? We often take our feelings as truth. We don't even question our instinctive reactions and responses. But when you learn to see beneath the surface, to look behind the language presenting the emotion, you'll discover that there's a thought process that generates the feelings you experience.

One of the ways to create massive success is to discover how your emotions affect who you are on a daily basis. Additionally, you should become aware of how the feelings you experienced are produced. This is a little-known, but extremely useful, key to producing positive results in your life.

When someone asks how your day is going your normal reaction might be to say, "Oh, it's okay" or "Not too bad." But there's little, if any, power in these responses. Instead, why not say, "Life is fantastic" or "Things are getting better and better." In this way, you'll be approaching your days from a much more empowering position. Your mind searches for the people, places and circumstances that will give you an absolutely fantastic day.

In the same way, your negative talk will have a discouraging effect on how you experience life. If you believe that things will not be too bad, then that's exactly what you will get. Things will be bad—just not too bad for you to manage. This is not a very beneficial way to experience life.

One way your language can either help or hurt you lies in the way that you typically speak of beneficial activities. Think about what a person usually says about doing something that would improve his or her life. You always hear people talk about what they "should" do. They say things like, "I should go get that book about sales from the local library this week." Or "I should sign up for that Asian cooking class this year." Or "I should wake up every morning 30 minutes earlier and just go for a jog." The problem with these statements is that a "should" doesn't contain the motivation necessary to create action.

A "should" is similar to a could, need or want. You know that when people use these words, they often never get around to doing what it is that they're talking about. When you say that you "should" do something, you are creating a perpetual state of anticipation. It's almost like saying that you are not going to do something that you want to do. You know this to be true, because how often do you really get around to doing something that you "should"?

If you're being truthful, you'll probably admit that most times you just don't do what you know you "should." A smoker knows that he or she should stop, but knowing that you should do something doesn't really make a difference by itself. How many smokers keep up the habit, year after year, thinking that one day in the future they will finally do what they know they should?

Let's look at a subtle way to shift your language that can make a huge difference in your performance. First, I would like to give all the credit on this one to Anthony Robbins, my mentor and model, for making this distinction. Robbins brilliantly talked about the concept of turning your "shoulds" into "musts." Let's take a look at what happens when you "must" do something. When you know you "must" complete a project, you will take the steps to get it done, period. You always have the energy, time and mindset to do what must be done.

For instance, if you're ever in a position where you don't have any food, you will do whatever it takes to get some. You might offer to do some daily work for cash or ask someone you know for a loan. If you were hungry enough, you might even find yourself going through trash cans just to survive. This is because eating is not simply something that you should do—it is a "must." You have to do it regularly and you know that. Your very life depends on completing that task.

If owning your own car was a "must" for you, you'd find a way to make that circumstance a reality. You might look for more ways to produce money and start saving that which you already have. You'd probably search the local classifieds or look for upcoming automobile auctions in the area. You would make it a point to achieve that goal. You would do so, simply because for you it is a "must," A "must" drives you; it moves you to take immediate action.

How you describe something determines the way that you conceptualize it. You would respond differently to a "should" than you would a "must" because the two words hold different meanings within your mind. They are separated into different categories, one for what you will do and another for things you probably won't.

Another word that can hold you back from success is "try." When you say that you will try to do something, it implies that you expect to fail. You can't really try to do anything. You either do it or you don't. There are certain tribal languages that don't even include a word for "try." This is because there's no such thing as trying. If you were sitting down right now and you wanted to stand up, you would either do it or you wouldn't. There would be no trying involved. If you put forth some effort and still found yourself sitting in the chair, you simply didn't stand up. If you did rise to your feet, then you didn't try. You stood.

When a person says that he or she is going to try, recognize that what he or she wants to do probably isn't going to happen. Using this word is a way of creating a loophole to excuse lack of effort and commitment. If you don't do what you intended to, you could always say, "Well, I tried." So trying is really an excuse, a way of saying, "I'm not fully committed to the task, but I want to believe that I am. Therefore, I'll try to do it and when I don't succeed, it won't be my fault."

One of the best things you can do to sustain your mindset of success is to eliminate the words "try" and "should" from your vocabulary. In doing this, you will actually make yourself accountable for producing the results that you want. You will, then, be much more careful about what you agree to and more committed to do exactly what you say you will do. When you avoid using "escape" words, you create an internal incentive to take action. Because you can no longer hide behind the "tries" and "shoulds," you will be the one held fully responsible for creating your own circumstances and results.

This way of looking at the world also gives you an incredible amount of power. It puts you directly in the driver's seat of your own life and destiny. Look at the words and phrases you use on a regular basis and remove those that do not empower you as a person. This involves replacing the negative parts of your vocabulary with words that make you feel better. For instance, the words discomfort, irritation, pain and anguish could all describe the same sensation. However, each one of those words will create a different experience within your mind and body. What if you decided to exchange the word pain for discomfort? When you think of something as being uncomfortable, you have an inner knowledge that it will eventually pass. In fact, uncomfortable circumstances can often build strength. You may actually come out better on the other end. When something is painful, however, it is much more difficult to get through. Pain is something that we just don't want and our minds will do almost anything to avoid it.

Anguish, however, is pain on steroids. It is something that permeates your entire being. Considering yourself to be in a state of anguish puts you at the mercy of whatever it is that you fear. You may think that words are no big deal, but sometimes a new set of words is all that you need to get your mind in an optimal state. If all we're talking about is words, wouldn't it serve you to use those that have a positive impact on your life? As you pursue your goals, you want to stack the deck in your favor. You MUST make an effort to use every possible skill-building tool at your disposal. Your choice of words is not a laughing matter. Use language to your benefit and you'll find yourself achieving much more than you ever imagined.

CHAPTER XXIV:

WORKSHEET

What phrases do you normally say to yourself that may inhibit your ability to perform well?

How can you reword these phrases to give you more power and control over your life?

When have you found yourself using the words "try" or "should" to describe activities that would be useful for you to complete?

What effect has verbalizing things in this way had on your ability to achieve positive results?

If you knew that completing these activities was a definite "must," how would your life change?

Why is using the word "try" a set-up for failure?

Why is it that you can't really "try" to do anything?

How does what you say affect the way you experience reality?

What words will you replace, starting right now?

CHAPTER XXV

Separating Yourself

In this chapter, we're going to discuss one of the secret keys to becoming great in any endeavor. Famed English physicist Isaac Newton once said, "I stand on the shoulders of giants," meaning that his discoveries were built on the accomplishments of others who came before him. We all achieve success in this way. If you develop a new way to market websites, you have been able to so because other people have paved the road to your success. Someone before you invented the Internet, the computer and even electricity. Without any of these things, you would not be able to even conceive of a website, much less develop anything to improve one's performance.

You may come up with a better way to close sales over the phone, but others before you invented the phone, the system that generates your leads and the direct sales model. Any person born today has already inherited countless inventions brought into reality by other people.

You don't have to reinvent the wheel, but in order to become great in your field, you must take the reins of creation and forge your own path. Too many people look at great performers in their field and try to emulate what they've done. As I mentioned earlier, it can be a really good thing to emulate those who have achieved what you want, but at some point you have to separate yourself from the pack.

Remember, you are an individual. No one else in this world has the same exact skills, abilities, talents or mindset that you do. When you are at your best, no one—and I mean no one—can outperform you. There is only one you, and you can do things that even the best in your chosen industry cannot.

Many people find it difficult to adopt this mindset. They fall prey to the mistaken assumption that they shouldn't be able to do what others before them have not. This idea is completely backwards. It is your place, your God-given right, to do things that others have yet to achieve—because there is no other you, and there will never *be* another you.

Let's say that you are in school and you want to become really good at writing essays. You've spotted another person in your class who seems to consistently get really good grades. You use his performance as your model and quickly start to improve your writing style. Soon, however, you reach a plateau, and it seems to you that you're just not cut out to develop the skills you want. But what you don't know is that you're actually holding yourself back from becoming a great writer. The person you are using as a model does very well. However, this is because he is using his own strengths to produce quality essays. At a certain point in your progress, you will find that following him no longer does you any good. Your mentor may have an aggressive style of writing that you just can't seem to get in touch with. But you may do very well at creating charismatic content that pulls at the hearts and minds of your readers. If you tried to merely copy the person that you admire, you would probably fall short in the end. You are not him and you can't do everything exactly the way he would. But look at the reverse of that last statement. The person who you admire also cannot do everything as well as you can. If you play to your strengths, you will achieve a level of success that is way beyond what this other person has ever had. Yes, his essays are powerful, but he cannot write with the level of finesse and elegance that you can. He has learned certain writing strategies that may be useful for you to acquire, but, at some point, you must enter your own realm of expertise in order to do really well.

Instead of following someone else's path, you must make the effort to blaze your own trail. You are on this planet for a reason, and that reason is you. You have an individual set of emotions, thoughts and interests. You can absolutely learn from the experiences of others, but you must also make it a point to live your own life, to do those things well that only you can do. This is the mark of greatness, the mark of someone who is truly fulfilling his or her purpose. So don't worry if you are not exactly like one of your "heroes." You were never meant to be exactly like anyone else. You are different, special and amazingly unique. You have your own path to create, your own mark to make on this wonderful world. So you should never be afraid of setting yourself apart from others. It is your right, your duty, to become the very best that only you can be.

One thing that deters us from becoming our best is the fear of failure. Most people just don't want to make mistakes. They want to be perfect in absolutely everything that they do. But you and I both know that achieving such an ideal life is virtually impossible. Fear of failure, therefore, will stop almost anyone from reaching an elite level of performance. In order to achieve success, you must be willing to be in the wrong many times before you develop the ability to do things right.

Then you have the person who's afraid of success. Believe it or not, many people fear success because they don't feel comfortable doing things that fall outside of their normal routines. These types of people will participate in self-sabotage, procrastination and any number of negative behaviors. The person who fears success doesn't want to disrupt his or her customary patterns. It is much easier to do less and feel comfortable than it is to perform at your best and face challenges directly. This is why the fear of success can cripple even the best of your intentions.

Each of these fears is merely an illusion. They don't actually exist in reality, which is why it's so important to develop a productive mindset.

How does a baby learn to walk? Some people say, "By practicing." But this is not really true. Remember that any baby will fall many times before he or she successfully stands. Therefore, the baby actually practices falling down more than he or she practices walking. If practice were the only thing needed to achieve success, everyone would be an expert at falling and almost no one would have learned how to walk. See, a baby conceptualizes his or her attempts at walking in a very particular way. Babies simply don't care if they fall while trying to walk. They delete unsuccessful attempts and only focus on how to do it better next time. This process occurs automatically, as a product of instinct. But somehow as we get the older, most of us tend to lose that spirit of just wanting to "go for it." Authority figures criticize us for being wrong, other children start to laugh at or ridicule us for doing things that fall outside of popular norms. Eventually, we find ourselves having less and less of that adventuresome spirit. We suppress that part of us that knows how to try something new.

The greatest inventors in history all found ways to go beyond what was done before. Sure, they learned from other people and so should you. But what they did was take those discoveries and put them together in ways that others had not thought of before. As a result, we now enjoy many products and technologies that make life a whole lot easier. So when you think about someone that you admire and want to be like, consider the fact that you can do even greater things than him or her.

A child will try to climb a tree in his backyard even though he may have never seen anyone do it before. However, most of us shrink at the thought of surpassing some of our greatest heroes. You may think, "Who am I to bring such wonderful things into the world?" But, in reality, who are you not to? Who are you *not to* take the ball and run even further? Who are you *not to* add your own unique perspective to the knowledge you've already acquired? The next move is yours. You may very well be the next person whom success-seekers of future generations come to admire.

When you break away from the pack, you are establishing yourself as a force to be reckoned with. You are demonstrating your true value and significance as an individual. Why rob the world of your true glory, simply because you're afraid to exceed others who have achieved greatness? Remember what we agreed on at the beginning of this book. You are writing your own story. Let me add to it this: You are writing your own story, not a chapter in someone else's life.

All of basketball legend Michael Jordan's teammates spoke of him as being both the first and the last. He was both the first person in the gym each day and the last one to leave. This type of dedication came through in his performance. He left "no stone unturned" and took no competition for granted. We can all take an important note from this man's personal biography. If you really want to stand out, you must be willing to go that extra mile. You must also allow yourself to be a little strange at times. Just look at the word "normal" and think about what it means. "Normal" is synonymous with words like "average," mediocre" and "commonplace." It describes the status quo—a "middle-of-the-road" person, situation or event. Because you're reading this book, chances are that you don't want this type of life.

What you have now may, in fact, be very normal. But you want to excel, to have an ideal relationship, lifestyle or career. You're tired of mediocrity and ready to do something about it. Some people believe that things would be great if they only learned to be like everybody else. But the average person is unfulfilled, unhappy or just scraping by when it comes to money. What's so great about that? It is often said that ordinary people do ordinary things; it's the "extra-ordinary" people, however, that do extraordinary things. If you want to do better than what you're doing in any area of life, you need to become a little weird. Others around you are probably doing about as well as you are. So, at least some of those people will find it odd when you start to act and think differently. That kind of response just goes along with the territory.

You can't worry too much about fitting in with those who are stuck someplace that you don't want to be. That kind of thinking will get you nowhere. In order to experience a higher quality of life, you must do some things that others simply won't. One of the things that can most inhibit your ability to succeed is the idea that you should stay within the crowd. It's time to step up your game, to take your performance up a few notches. All you need to think about is becoming the very best "you" that you can be. You don't need to meet your neighbors' standards, social limitations or cultural superstitions. Part of becoming truly successful on all levels, therefore, involves separating yourself from other people—not in a way that is arrogant or conceited, but in a manner that respects your true calling as an individual. See, you can imitate anyone else in the world, but you can only become the very best at being yourself. Your own individual mind is, in fact, one of the only things that no one can ever corrupt or take from you without your permission.

CHAPTER XXV:

WORKSHEET

What does the phrase "Stand on the shoulders of giants" mean?

Why is it that no one can outperform you at your best?

What skills, abilities or ideas do you have that can further the achievements of someone whom you admire?

How will improving upon the work of your heroes benefit future generations?

How can the fear of failure sabotage your greatness?

What about the fear of success?

Why do many of us lose our adventuresome spirit as we get older?

How did people create some of the most useful inventions at our disposal today?

Why is it both your right and duty to separate yourself from the pack?

CHAPTER XXVI

Get Excited

The next principle deals with the way you approach your daily life. It's important that you go into the world with energy, with an attitude that says, "Today is a new leg of my journey and it's going to be a wonderful ride." You want to approach each day with enthusiasm and passion. Passion is an important part of really getting the best out of whatever you do. There's no honor in tiptoeing through life, whispering your thoughts and hoping not to be noticed. Whatever you send out into the universe will return to you. Therefore, it is utterly important that you pursue your goals with high levels of energy and zeal.

Think about when you do something in a lackluster fashion. Maybe you had a certain task to complete at one time, but you really couldn't muster up the enthusiasm or energy to follow it through well. How often will you do your very best when you're in that particular state of mind? Obviously, the answer is not very often.

However, when you're really passionate about doing something, you perform better, think clearer, and have an all-around higher quality of experience. One of the little-known keys to achieving anything worthwhile lies in getting really excited about what you're doing and enjoying the process.

When you wake up, notice how you routinely approach the day. Do you get up with a frown on your face, thinking about the money that you don't have, the kids that don't listen and the house you haven't cleaned? If you have these things on your mind when you wake up, it is likely that they will continue to haunt you throughout the day. On the other hand, if you get up and start things out with a big smile, feeling absolutely enthusiastic about the day to come, you'll probably find yourself being more productive and satisfied with whatever you do. Your state of mind determines how you will perform.

When you consistently feel bad, it's easy for everything to just fall apart. This is a very simple concept, yet it is one that many people overlook when pursuing their goals. So you need to get yourself feeling really good and powerful as soon as possible. Then, work at keeping and improving your energy levels high throughout the day.

People who are really excited about life have a certain charisma, don't they? They exude a positive energy that infects those people they encounter. This is why success-minded people love to be around others who are passionate. When you associate with someone who's simply on fire, your mood improves by association. People who are passionate about their goals also go after more of what they want. Many of us lose out because we simply don't ask for what we really desire. Excitement, however, fills you with a persistent need to make the best of your circumstances. You don't have time to worry about the naysayers and other people who approach you in a negative fashion. That energy fuels you. It ignites that inner sense of wanting to explore life and get the most of what you experience. A high level of enthusiasm is extremely beneficial to both your education and growth. So you must learn how to bring an intense feeling of enthusiasm into your everyday life. You'll improve, get more out of your environment and develop better relationships with people.

It can be easy sometimes to get caught up in a rut. It may start to feel like you're just doing the same things every day, without seeing the results that you hoped for. Often, when it seems that we're not getting enough out of daily life, it's because we simply don't intend to. You've got to aim for something each day—to try to do things just a little better or smarter. You want to get excited about your goals, of course, but you can find other ways to generate enthusiasm for your days as well. You can get inspiration from the stories of other people. Perhaps you could start your days by reading from the biography of someone who has gotten to the level of achievement that you wish to reach. Doing this is bound to get you going in good mental and emotional states. You'll then take that positive attitude into whatever you do that day.

It's also okay to put some forethought into how you will generate the passion and enthusiasm you need. You can make a plan each night to do things that give you a sense of excitement during the day ahead.

The important thing is to you keep your mind focused on what it is that you plan to create. Moreover, you will be utilizing the positive aspects of your desired outcome to generate an ongoing sense of enthusiasm. It can be hard to continue pursuing your dreams when you're just doing the "grunt work," day-in and day-out. You have to find a way to continue experiencing the joys of having what you want. Congratulate yourself for small wins. Remember that Rome wasn't built in a day. There's no reason to avoid giving yourself expressions of approval. Almost nothing is too small, as long as it moves you toward your goals. Don't worry about trying to hold self-praise in reserve. What would you be saving it for anyway? Don't just celebrate little victories, look for them. Doing so incorporates a lot of the action steps discussed in this book. It causes you to be thankful, remain positive, focus on the good and build up momentum. It's not conceited to pat yourself on the back when you deserve it. In fact, it would be careless not to do so. When you don't appreciate your own accomplishments, you commit an act of neglect against yourself.

The need to wake up with an ongoing smile on your face is crucial to achieving mastery in any area of your life. When I make this statement at my events, a lot of people say, "But Anthony, how can I begin a day with a smile if everything around me is falling apart? How can I remember to forget my problems and act like everything is okay?" If you, too, are thinking this, I have a very simple yet highly effective solution.

A few years back, I came across the saying "Begin each day as if it were on purpose," by Mary Anne Radmacher. Instantly amazed by this blunt yet empowering statement, I felt my spirit of play kick in. I began to evaluate the applicability and feasibility of this saying on my own life. As Anthony Robbins says, the process of evaluation is nothing but asking yourself a series of questions. So I began my evaluation journey, if you will. What does it mean to begin each day as if it were on purpose? How can I begin a day over which I have no control? Well, maybe by setting an alarm? Okay, but still, even if I make it a ritual to get up at a certain time, how can I remember to begin my day with a smile? Maybe writing the word "smile" on a small piece of paper to read every single morning would help. But why would I want to write such a *phenomenal* word on a small piece of paper? Is the keyword to designing the best quality of my own life not worth being engraved on a huge billboard?

Suddenly it hit me! I should print this word on paper large enough that that I could never miss it. Guess what? I still have that banner hanging from the ceiling above my bed in such a position that the minute I open my eyes, I cannot miss reading it! Over the years, in fact, I began to modify it as my knowledge of and fascination with the world of personal development grew deeper. Now that same huge banner proudly reads:

"Dear Anthony,

I was here impatiently waiting for you to wake up. Now that you're up, remember that if you cannot control the events around you, you can surely control how you feel about them with a huge smile. Your life, your choice!

Sincerely,

Your Day"

I invite you to do the same if you're serious about having a premium quality of life. You must take charge of own your success. You have to show your belief systems, thoughts and habits exactly who is in charge. But doing this can be more challenging than it seems. If you've learned to externalize your power—assigning responsibility for your life to outside forces—it may feel like you have no control over what happens. But remember these things: Your past does not determine your future, and it's not about where you start, but how you finish.

You no longer have to accept the roles, status or position that life gave you. In order to get to that next level, however, you must make an investment in yourself and your future. It's worth saying over and over again: "You have to do something different in order to get something different." You must step out into some uncharted territory. This doesn't mean that you should gamble with your life. I'm not telling you to get reckless and follow every trend that passes by. But in order to become successful in any area of life, you are required to take the appropriate risks. The key to navigating these risks successfully lies within you. You have to go out to the end of the rainbow and grab your pot of gold. It's yours for the taking. All you have to do is keep going and, eventually, you'll get there.

Not only must you expect to win in the game of life, but you need to demand it. And don't be afraid to get out of your head and into your heart. Passion is a very powerful tool for creating positive change. In fact, it is a prerequisite to creating a life of purpose and fulfillment. Know that you can beat the odds. Don't let others' skepticism and negative predictions hold you back. As famed Irish playwright George Bernard Shaw once said, "People who say it cannot be done should not interrupt those who are doing it."

You were created as an individual and there are no accidents in the universe. You are here to manifest something great that is inside of you right now. So you might as well get out there, pull up your sleeves and give it all you got. Do so for yourself and the rest of the world. You are a messenger, here to shine upon others the light that was placed within you at birth. The body and mind are simply your tools of communication. Remember that you stand on the shoulders of giants. Others who came before you have left their legacies for you to build upon, and you are also here to lay the groundwork for coming generations. So, do your part. The very fate of this world depends upon it. No one else can take over your responsibility to the universe. No one can do your job. You have a distinct place within this wonderful mosaic called life. It's yours and yours alone.

If you have children or other people who look up to you, then this point is especially important. You can try to teach kids using logic and reason, expressed verbally. But, the truth is that children primarily learn from example. Many people overlook this very obvious fact. Think of the scatter-brained parents who simply don't understand why their kids won't pay attention to anything worthwhile. Or, the shiftless adult who criticizes his kids for not participating in more outdoor activities. The old parental adage goes, "Do as I say, not as I do"—but that saying is built entirely on faulty logic. People, children included, are always paying attention to what you do, not what you say. It's your actions, not your words, that make a lasting and influential mark on others. It's time for you to show life that you're serious. If you take a lackluster approach to working toward your own success, reality will not compensate for what you have neglected to do. Nobody will show up to carry you the rest of the way. It's very easy to lose perspective, to assume that the opportunities you now have will always be there. There really is no other time, though, but now. It's likely that whatever you put off doing today will seem just as, if not more, difficult for you to complete tomorrow. There is much truth to the old saying that goes, "Tomorrow never comes." It really doesn't. All you have is a continuous series of present moments.

Think about something that you did in the past. At the moment it happened, it was not the past, but the present. Mistakes from your past may come back to haunt you, but you must work on resolving them now. There is no other time to do it. If you actually get around to doing something tomorrow, it won't be tomorrow when it's done. It will be now. So, putting things off for the future is really a futile practice. You're simply wasting your precious moments, one by one.

This is not to take away from the importance of preparation. You should definitely learn to swim before jumping into the deep end of any pool. This could mean taking the time to learn and practice some communication skills before making that big presentation. It could mean setting aside twenty dollars each week for a dream cruise that departs two years from now. But you must do these things now—not tomorrow, next week or next month.

Many people are not armed with the knowledge that you're attaining right now from reading this book. Most are simply waiting around for their circumstances in life to change, but for some reason you were drawn to this material, and I'm honored and grateful to be sharing with you all this knowledge that has helped me personally and thousands of others to reinvent their lives. A part of you knows that something more is out there waiting for you. The possibilities are endless once you start to develop the power of your mind. You've taken the first step toward creating a life that's better than anything you've experienced before, and again, I'm truly honored to be serving you and helping you get there.

Don't let your environment dictate what you should be, have, do or produce. An empty bank account doesn't mean that you're poor. It's just a reflection of what you used to do. Just because you've never known a person of your gender or race who has accomplished what you want doesn't mean that you can't be the first. People often conform to their surroundings, in both positive and negative ways. But what you see does not indicate your true potential.

Each day, you must purposefully decide to seek out the people, places and things that will help you achieve your ultimate goal. It is essential that you also *follow through* with this process every day. This is about choosing your future, creating a life that's made just for you. What task could be more admirable, more honorable, and more authentic? Nothing would fulfill you more than realizing your own inner greatness. This is what we're here to do; this is the reason that you and I have crossed paths at this particular moment in time.

It's important that you work at surrounding yourself with others who are doing what you want to do. People pass bad ideas between one another quicker than the common cold. There's something in modern psychology known as a meme, or a mind virus. As the name implies, these are thoughts and beliefs that spread throughout a particular social system. That system could be your family of origin, local community, nation or private group. If these thought patterns are negative, they can wreak havoc on an individual's mental state, just as organic disease works to destroy the physical body. Many of these ideas are very restrictive in nature and they work behind the scenes, destroying people from the inside-out. The problem is that we don't usually feel comfortable going beyond the limitations of our social groups. Studies show that you will likely become obese if most of your friends are overweight. A person's annual earnings will probably be within $2,000 to $3,000 of the earnings of those closest to him. We are all affected. The real question is: Who are you allowing to influence your behavior—those who are doing well or others who have resigned themselves to living a life of disappointment and despair? When you get down to it, poverty, inferiority, fear and apprehension are all mindsets. These mental attitudes are like spells that capture and distort a person's good sensibilities. So, you have to break through that. You have to wake yourself out of the trance into which possibly well-meaning people led you years ago.

Make no mistake about it; you are making a dramatic adjustment to the course of your life. To do that, you must have that internal drive, that energy and life-force that pushes you through tough times. At the start of each day, take a few moments to really get yourself "pumped up." This alone will increase your likelihood of success in any area of life.

Don't look back with regret over any time you've wasted in the past. Those moments are gone, never to return. Now is the perfect time to move toward a higher calling. You have to get yourself together, let go of old disappointments and put your very best out on the table. You've got some really great things to bring into this world, and you want to live from a position of power, not one of victimhood.

Hold the image of your final success in your mind. If you want a more intimate marriage, picture you and your spouse having tender moments—sharing, being close, feeling just like you did in the beginning. If you want to get a better job, walk, talk, move and speak as thought it's already yours. Some of my clients carry around pictures of their goals to focus on at different points through the day. Others have affirmative statements written on small index cards. Do whatever is necessary to remind yourself of where you're going. Today's world is filled with so many distractions that it can sometimes be very difficult to keep your eye on the prize. This is why it's good to intentionally put things in your way that revivify that sense of purpose and commitment. You might put together what's known as a vision board. This would be a poster board or frame filled with images and photographs of your desired lifestyle. The great thing about a vision board is that it can encompass every area of your life. You can conceptualize your ideal relationship, places you'd like to go, your perfect home, your ideal body and your desired income level. This allows you to get really creative in expressing your dreams. You need to be able to see what you want every day. Doing so will ingrain those images within your subconscious mind. It will then guide you to the resources and opportunities you need to make your physical life match the one you're already living inside of your head. Seeing yourself having what it is that you want is very important. You must get your subconscious comfortable with the idea that this new lifestyle is yours.

You're the only one who can make it happen. Support from others is a great resource if you can get it. But no one is going to care about your dreams the way you do. Nobody else has the same insight, experiences and perspective that you have. You have to spend time working on yourself and investing in the achievement of your goals every single day.

Don't let the fear of failure hold you back. Make it a point to fail forward, to look at everything that happens as a learning opportunity. You must make a commitment to keep going after what you want, over and over, until there's a break-through and you make it happen. Sometimes life will knock you down. Just as things are going well, something can come out of nowhere and blindside you. When that happens, it's your job to get up and go after it even stronger and harder. Make sure that you take first things first. Don't let yourself get too distracted by nonessential activities, and keep a keen eye on what's important. You know what it is you need to do, and now it's time to get busy. Sometimes we busy ourselves with things that have little or no importance in order to avoid the discomfort of moving forward. Don't let your mind play this kind of trick on you. Get the significant things out of your way first. Then, if you still wish to, you can move on to more trivial matters.

Make this word a part of your vocabulary: yet. You haven't really failed at anything. You just haven't learned how to do it, yet. You didn't fail at motivating your kids; you simply haven't found the way to do it yet. You didn't fail at becoming an excellent presenter. It's just that there are some things you haven't yet learned how to do. See, the word failure describes something that has come to an end. But using the word "Yet" means that you're still open to possibilities. Whatever it is that you want, you must always keep in mind that it's possible. It's possible to have the life of your dreams, to create the circumstances to make it possible, to develop the skills and achieve the goals that you desire. Get excited about the new life you're creating, for the best is yet to come!

CHAPTER XXVI:

WORKSHEET

What are some of your long-term goals?

What are the initial reasons you became enthusiastic about these objectives?

Imagine that you've achieved what it is that you want. How does it feel to be successful?

What images, sounds, smells or tastes come to mind?

What would happen if you revisited these thoughts and sensations as you awoke each day?

If you did this regularly throughout the day, how would your attitude be affected?

How do children accomplish something new successfully, like walking or riding a bicycle, even though they fail at doing so many times before learning?

How can you use this principle to help you maintain a positive attitude?

Why is it good to model your actions on those of others who have achieved success?

How can you remind yourself to begin each day as if it were on purpose?

If you cannot control events around you, what could you control?

CHAPTER XXVII

Operate with Integrity

If you want to become truly successful, you must practice being a person of integrity—there's no way around it. Of course, there are many dishonest people who have made a lot of money. But those people are not successful in the truest sense. I think that self-help pioneer Earl Nightingale put it best. He describes success as the progressive realization of a worthy ideal. Your personal worth should not be determined by your number of material possessions. It rests in your character, personality and moral code.

To operate with integrity, you must avoid cheating people at all costs. There may be times when it would be easier to take a shortcut than to do the right thing. But you don't want to live your life knowing that you've been the direct cause of others' misfortune. In the end, it would harm the way you feel about yourself. Whether you perceive the damage or not, cheating others will slowly dismantle your self-esteem from the inside out.

Cheating others is simply not the way to go, as either a short or long-term solution. You may get away with it for a while. But, eventually, people will get an intuitive sense that you are not to be trusted. They'll start to feel like you only have your own interests in mind. Over time, you will develop a bad reputation and people will feel uncomfortable dealing with you. When you work together with others, insist on creating only win-win scenarios. Things will always work out best when you offer someone else a benefit for doing what it is that you wish. Many people operate according to a win-lose, lose-win or lose-lose mentality. This means that they try to get the upper hand, play the role of victim, or set things up so that no one ends up getting what they want.

Any interaction, whether professional or personal, is an exchange of value. You will get much more of what you want by giving others what they desire in return. This is really the best way to go about things. Everyone ends up happy, satisfied and committed to strengthening the relationship. What I'm saying is that you should always think about what you are projecting or offering to other people. Value is, actually, the universal means of exchange. This is true even in friendships. Why do you prefer to think of one person as a friend and another as a mere acquaintance? The friend gives you more personal value. He or she may listen to your grievances or have common experiences that you can relate to. You appreciate a friend on a much more intimate level than you do most people. An acquaintance, on the other hand, is simply someone you know. You don't have the same type of relationship with him or her, because the value exchange is much less.

We live in a world full of other human beings. At some point, getting what we want will require interacting with other people and getting their assistance. This is why it's important that you become a person who offers value to others. When you do this, people will offer you support and help in more ways than you could ever imagine.

One of the greatest ways to operate with integrity is to be happy for others' successes. When someone you know accomplishes something big, congratulate him or her and get excited for his or her good-fortune. This will condition your mind to believe that success is a good thing and that there is more than enough to go around. When you practice being happy for others, you take a big step toward drawing positive things into your own life.

Feeling jealous or envious when others do well, however, will create exactly the opposite effect. By having that sort of attitude, you would actually be rejecting all of the wonderful things that could come into your life. The jealous person operates from the mindset of scarcity. He or she believes that there just isn't enough to go around. When one person achieves something, the jealous person feels as if that accomplishment is somehow taking away from his or her chances to succeed. Thinking in this way makes it very hard for your mind to find valuable opportunities.

Many people believe that success comes as a result of wanting things and taking the physical actions to achieve them. The truth is, however, that you don't get what you *want* out of life; you get what you *are*. Your own character has an incredible impact on how you perform and what you accomplish. Therefore, it serves you to hold yourself to a high moral standard. This point cannot be stressed enough. Your environment and your circumstances are a reflection of who you are on the inside. As the ancient saying goes, "As within, so without." You cannot produce anything that exceeds the limits of your own personality and character. When you take away all the flashy clothes, cars and other material possessions, all you have left is you. You are the center of your own universe, and if you are not solid, your world will soon crumble.

A big part of integrity lies in being honest. A liar is always on edge. He has to constantly monitor his deceptions so other people don't figure out what's going on. When you're truthful about your intentions, however, you don't have to feel tense and uneasy about what you say. Committing yourself to being honest, regardless of what the potential outcome may be, says wonderful things about who you are.

You may be tempted to stretch the truth when you're going for a job or getting into a relationship—but doing that would put you in a constant state of anxiety, as you will worry that you will eventually be exposed. If you always represent yourself honestly, however, you have nothing to fear. When you go for that new job, it's best to be truthful about your skills, motivations and abilities. It is then the employer's responsibility to choose whether to hire you. If you get the job, you don't have to feel guilty about not being able to perform certain tasks. You were upfront from the very beginning and your boss selected you "as-is."

In a new relationship, people are trying to figure out whether they relate well to each other. This cannot happen unless both people are honest from the very beginning. There is nothing to gain by presenting a false persona to the other person. As time goes by, the real you will come to the surface and your partner will feel betrayed, confused and then misled. But if you're truthful from the start, it gives you an actual chance to find romantic love. A good relationship cannot be based upon lies. If it's not really going to work out, then you and the other person have a right to know.

One of the best ways you can demonstrate that you're a person of integrity is by keeping your word. People will always be examining you, looking for clues about your character and personality. When you habitually back out of agreements, it says something negative about you. Others will soon learn that you are not to be taken seriously and avoid cooperating with you on important issues. If you stand by what you say, however, you will make the opposite impression. You will come to be known as one whom others can trust and whose words are as "good as gold." People like to feel secure. They want to know that the agreements they make with others will stand. If you want to separate yourself from the pack, all you have to do is keep your promises. Many people in today's world don't.

Here's a good rule to live by. Promise something to another person only if you are fully capable of and committed to keeping your word. If you are not completely dedicated to doing what you are asked, simply don't agree to it. You do have the right to refuse any request. Many of us find it difficult to say no to people we're acquainted with. However, this is the best way to respond when you're really not willing to do what's asked. People will respect you more in the end, knowing that you'll only make a promise that you are committed to keeping.

CHAPTER XXVII:

WORKSHEET

In what areas of your life does it seem like you could receive a short-term benefit by being unfair to others?

How would doing this impact your reputation in that area over time?

Why must it be a high priority to think "win-win" when dealing with others?

Why is it important for you to celebrate others' successes?

What does the mind learn from jealousy and envy?

Why does a deceptive person have to stay "on guard?"

Why must you represent yourself truthfully when applying for a job or position?

What happens when someone bases his or her romantic relationship on a made-up persona?

What kind of reputation do you build by not keeping your word?

How does doing what you promise build trust?

What is it best to do when you know that you're really not committed to following through on complying with another's request?

CHAPTER XXVIII

Fill Your Life with Positivity

In order to achieve your dreams, it is important that you surround yourself with an atmosphere of positivity. You are, of course, the captain of your ship. You alone are responsible for producing the results that you want, but your environment still has a huge impact on your ability to succeed.

We human beings are social animals by nature. We have an intuitive need to interact with one another. In order to survive, we develop communities and establish social norms. This helps us to create a safe and stable environment in which we may live, work and play. We are encouraged to follow, and go along with, behaviors that are most prevalent in our society. The bad thing about following the crowd is that doing so can limit you in many ways. When you want to do more than others around you, there's an instinctive force that tries to pull you back. Most of us desire to become just "one of the bunch" and avoid activities that might cause others to feel bad. At different stages of growth and development, we have different needs to fulfill. As young children, we desperately want to belong and be accepted by peers. But this need often extends into adult life, where we find ourselves doing whatever it takes to be a part of the "popular" crowd.

Internal barriers may inhibit you from creating a better quality of life. Subconsciously, you may believe that developing a higher level of awareness means that you'll start judging those who are dear to you. However, water seeks its own level and so does intelligence. Sometimes, it can feel like there's an invisible force that's just trying to push you down to a lower level of performance. That's why it can be so hard to fulfill your dreams when people around you don't want anything out of life. They won't be able to understand why you want to have and become more. Fishermen have observed what happens when a bunch of crabs are caught and put into a bucket. When one crab tries to climb out, the others will quickly pull him back down. The "crab in the bucket phenomenon" applies to people, too. Some people you know will actually try to bring you down, so that they can continue dealing with you on a comfortable level.

Many people do this without any conscious awareness of their behavior. They have psychologically repressed their true intentions. These types of people are very persistent, as they actually feel as though they're looking out for your best interests. This does not change the fact, however, that you're being sabotaged from achieving your goals.

There are also other, more concrete, parts of your surroundings that can hold you back. Perhaps you used to play video games for four hours a day. Maybe you watched TV with friends or family members during most of your free time. But now that you have established a clear purpose and set of goals, you have become committed to living in a more productive manner. You might decide to sell the TV or keep your video game play down to a minimum, but people with whom you did these activities are still very involved in them. Your friends will still come over to play video games. Family members will draw your attention to unimportant things on television. People will come by and ask you to go out with them and participate in any number of time-wasting distractions. Just because you've decided to improve your life doesn't mean that everyone else around you has made a similar decision. You will feel some resistance to whatever you are trying to achieve. Others will definitely try to pull you back into the mainstream crowd. After all, you were once a member of the same groups that you are now surpassing.

You can't move forward while holding onto your past limitations. Self help expert Bob Proctor says that a person who earns $50,000 a year probably doesn't do so because that's exactly what he wants. He makes $50,000 because he doesn't know how to earn $150,000. You performed the way that you did in the past because that's what you knew how to do back then. As you continue to learn and grow, however, you will become capable of doing more with your life than ever before. In fact, it will become necessary for you to improve. Once your mind has stretched past its former limits, you won't be able to think as you did before. You will have an expanded view of reality, one that operates according to your new level of understanding.

You need to be very deliberate about whom you spend your time with. There are countless of people in the world who can help you develop whatever lifestyle you choose. Why should you waste any time trying to hold on to others who simply add no value to your situation? Of course certain people, like family members, are especially hard to avoid. If you have relatives who are cynical and negative, however, you have to be very careful about how you spend your time with them. It may be helpful for you to visit these people only at family gatherings. You might want to just avoid them all together. I don't know exactly what makes sense for you, but it's essential that you purposefully put yourself around people who add value to your life.

We're often much too connected to the flaws of people we know. What happens when you see someone doing something that you are sure is bad for him or her? Don't you kind of want to step in and make things right? Each person you meet, however, is on his or her own path. People progress at their own individual rates of improvement. It may take someone you know years to reach the level of development that you are at right now, but that pace is just right for him or her.

Associate with people who empower you, who encourage you and help you grow. You may say, "I can help others around me get better and we'll all succeed together." You cannot change anyone, however, but yourself. Making your dreams a reality takes a lot of effort and mental energy. You don't have any time to deal with anyone else's limitations. It's hard enough developing yourself, changing your own limiting beliefs into those that empower you.

Unfortunately, we live in a society based on the premise of competition. People are always trying to outdo one another. This ideology creates a brand of individuals known as "haters." Haters are people who simply don't want you to get ahead. They will do everything possible to discredit you, discourage you and keep you from going for whatever it is that you want. Haters feel like your success takes away from their own achievements, so they will systematically break down even your best intentions. You want to recognize the haters in your world and avoid them at all cost. They will do absolutely nothing but bring you down.

Sometimes we associate with people simply by chance. They enter our lives in a coincidental fashion and we receive them openly, without any evaluation. Over time, these people can start to affect the way we behave. Not everyone who comes into your life is good for you. Not every person who extends the hand of friendship does so with the best of intentions. You should be very selective about who you associate with, as your choices will have a huge impact on how well you perform.

Remember that "birds of a feather flock together." The longer that you associate with someone, the more influence that person will have on your life. I once heard it said that "if your nine best friends are broke, it won't be long before you're number ten." Negative people will bring you down, drain your energy and incrementally destroy your dreams. Positive people, on the other hand, will build you up, encourage you to get more out of life and help you succeed. It's not hard to see why it is so beneficial for you to hang out with success-minded individuals.

In order to become really successful, you'll probably need some coaching. Even the greatest producers in history have had other people in their lives from whom they sought guidance and support. Getting a personal coach or mentor is one of the best ways to achieve your dreams. Your success may lie in finding this kind of help. A mentor is someone who can guide you through the process of achieving your dreams. He or she will be someone who has specialized knowledge in your particular area of interest. Many times, we believe that we should just be able to do whatever we want all by ourselves. We often don't think of looking to a qualified outside advisor for help. But a mentor can help you answer important questions about how to achieve your individual goals. There are times when all of us need a little advice. If you can develop a relationship with someone who has been where you want to go, you'll be able to learn in ways that most people never imagine.

There are many things to look for when selecting a mentor. First, you can choose someone who's an expert in your chosen field. Or, you may select someone who's gone from where you are to where you want to be. A person like this can be an enormous asset to your life. He or she has a proven plan of achievement that relates directly to your goals. You must also look for someone who's willing to help you. The schedules of some successful people may be too full for them to take on any private tutoring.

Many experienced people, however, are willing to help those with similar interests. All you have to do is ask. The worse that anyone can say is no. But if you make the effort—if you contact people who can help you achieve your goals—I bet you'll be surprised at the number of positive responses you'll get. Successful people have been exactly where you are, after all. They have created lofty goals, been discouraged by others and looked for people to learn from. For this reason, many successful people will be more than willing to steer you toward success.

There are many other ways to surround yourself with positivity. If you want to buy a bigger home, then you need to saturate your mind with images of your goal. You may want to cut out, from magazines and books, pictures of the kind of house that you want to live in. Make sure to put them up in places that you will see several times a day. You can post the pictures above your bed or on the bathroom mirror, refrigerator or hallway wall. Just make sure to put a picture of your goal someplace you'll be sure to pass by every day.

Make it a point to listen to positive messages every day. Much of the mainstream media is aimed at broadcasting tales of woe and despair. Advertisers, along with radio and television producers, have built many campaigns centered around sensationalism. Today's news has become less about reporting facts and more about getting you to watch the latest broadcast. This is one of the reasons you must deliberately choose what comes into your mind.

Have you ever noticed that most of a typical news report is spent describing some horrible event or warning you of forthcoming danger? This is because one of our primary instinctual drivers is fear. See, reporters know that if all they talked about was good cheer and peace on earth, many people wouldn't feel compelled to watch. When you hear a sound bite that says, "Here are five things that threaten your life!" or "Find out how someone can steal all of your money!" you are almost obligated to tune in. Because of our need to avoid pain, commercial interests can use fear as a behavior-modifying tool.

These factors, and many others, cause people to get caught up in an extremely negative mindset. They doubt anyone and anything that does not fit into their pre-programmed version of reality. They haven't yet found a way to surpass their previous limitations and become positive about life. Take a minute to listen to other people's language and you will understand exactly what I mean. You might hear one person say, "Why is he so happy all of the time?" or "What the heck is she smiling about?"

It's amazing how some people are simply addicted to feeling bad. There are people who will get angry at you for choosing to feel good about your life, and that's a fact. You will be criticized for pursuing the dreams they never dared to pursue. Even those who you love and respect may try to discourage you at times, in unexpected ways. A parent may tell you about the low percentage of people who succeed in your chosen field. A spouse may subtly preach about the benefits of getting a so-called "real job." You may find a friend starting to ridicule you, all in the spirit of "fun." Negativity has many forms, and any of them may manifest themselves while you travel your chosen path.

Your breaking out of your comfort zone and current conditions is going to scare some people. Many will see your success as a painful reminder of what they could have accomplished, but didn't. Negative messages are around you all of the time. If you don't make it a point to intentionally feed your mind with positive suggestions, you can easily fall prey to momentary doom and gloom.

How you treat yourself also can have an effect on your mental and emotional state. Remember that you are a special and talented individual, worthy of getting whatever it is that you want to achieve. You deserve the very best and you have the right to care about and for yourself. Until you can do this, however, you are not likely to enjoy a better quality of life.

The way you treat yourself says a great deal about what you consider yourself to be worth. After all, if you had the most valuable item on earth, would you keep it under the kitchen sink or behind the bathroom toilet? I think not. It's funny because many of us have difficulty treating ourselves with the same consideration that we do others. Many people will give special attention to friends and family, yet not attend to their own needs. You cannot leave yourself out of the picture. You must make it a priority to care for yourself.

How you respond to other people can indicate what you think you deserve. Do you have a tough time accepting compliments? If so, you may have a self-image problem and believe you are not worthy of receiving praise. When someone offers you a kind word, it's okay to simply accept it and thank that person for the comment. If you want to get ahead, you must start believing that you are an individual of value. Know that you deserve to receive as well as give.

Consider how someone in your desired position would dress, walk and act. Now, look at how you perform the same behaviors on a daily basis. Do you dress down, meaning you habitually maintain a sloppy and unkempt appearance? This may mean that you do not feel deserving of being your ideal self. Or you may be in the habit of not doing nice things for yourself. You feel unworthy of buying yourself that new outfit that would help you "look the part."

Do you spend time and money on things you enjoy? Or do you mostly succumb to the whims and wishes of others around you? Do you speak up when choosing where to eat or go out? Or do you sit back and let others make all of the decisions? The answers to these questions will help you figure out how much you really believe you are worth in relation to others.

Have you ever noticed that the person who cowers to people and has a hard time speaking often gets a lot of criticism from others? Conversely, those who stand strong, exuding confidence and self-assurance, seem to get the most respect. This doesn't happen simply by a chance. The person who shrinks from people projects that he does not expect to be treated well. Some people pick up on this cue and respond to it by giving him exactly what he wants. Someone who thinks very well of herself, however, gets the opposite response. Others instinctively recognize her confidence, poise and charisma, so she is also treated exactly as she expects to be.

Almost everything you do tells a story. Those stories that you tell yourself on a daily basis create who it is that you are. Are you living out the story of a martyr, someone who is persecuted and reviled without cause? Are you living the life of an outcast who never gets his one big break? Are you playing the role of victim, one who is constantly oppressed by others? The way you treat yourself is a good indicator of how the rest of the world will receive you. What you believe is what you get. Your subconscious mind will make sure that what you perceive on the inside matches what you project onto the outside world. And since people will respond to you in the way you treat yourself, your thoughts eventually become your reality. You need to have a solid, intentional plan, therefore, for treating yourself well every single day.

Remember what I said earlier about the way that most people perceived problems? They view difficulties as being pervasive, overwhelming and everlasting. This means that they see the problem as affecting every part of their lives, being too large to manage and unyielding. But I want you to remember that there is always a way out. Think about the challenges you may have had as a child. Maybe you were trying to learn math or ride a bike. You worked at it over and over again without success. Back then, those things may have seemed like huge problems, unsolvable ones. As you look back now, however, you can see that those issues have meant very little to your overall experience of life. You have a better perspective and a more complete view of reality now. Think of your life at this moment. Your current difficulties may seem entirely insignificant in the future. Ten years from now you may look back and realize that your problems at this moment are not very real.

You found ways to get through past problems. If you hadn't, you would not be here today. Your life would not be as good or well-organized as it is. You will get through today's problems in the same way. There's always a way. There's always some avenue that will take you to wherever you want to be.

The problems of your younger days held you back for some very specific reasons. You were thinking with the mentality that you had developed up until that point. Now, your former difficulties have become obsolete because you are looking at them from a higher level of understanding. Therefore, it stands to reason that in the future the problems of today will be just as out-of-date and irrelevant.

I want you to imagine yourself in the future. Take yourself five or ten years into the future and look back on your life right now. Think about what you were going through and how you perceived those problems to be real. But as you are there, now, in the future, you can look back and maybe even laugh about what you went through in the past. Now, come back to the present moment and think about what you've learned. Just remember that it's probably not that serious and never was. Self-improvement author Richard Carlson put it simply: "Don't sweat the small stuff—and it's all small stuff." Have you ever met an elderly person who never seems to get as upset or out of sorts as other people? It's likely because this person has seen and done it all. Experience has shown him or her how to relax and take things in stride. Think about the fact that there will be a time when you will likely feel the same way. Your biggest challenges won't seem nearly as insurmountable in a few years.

However, you also encounter those older people who seem to get angry all of the time. They're grumpy, crotchety and just disappointed with life in general. They never learned to let go of difficulties, no matter how large or small. They held on to the every little annoyance until being annoyed became the very essence of their lives. If you want to produce quality results, you have to get positive about life. As renowned British statesman and author Winston Churchill said, "Attitude is the little thing that makes a big difference."

CHAPTER XXVIII:

WORKSHEET

What does being positive mean to you?

What are some qualities you have perceived in happy and successful people that could help you maintain a positive attitude?

What are some acts of kindness you can start undertaking for others, to put out into the world what you want to receive?

Write down at least 5 positive things that happened to you last week.

What are some things that turned out well for you today?

Think about someone you know now who has affected your life in a positive way. Commit to taking time this week to express your gratitude to this person. Write what you will say here.

What are some ways you will now take better care of yourself?

Which of your current "problems" are you likely to laugh about in the future?

How does your personal story affect the way that others act toward you?

What things that you really enjoy will you dedicate yourself to do this week?

CHAPTER XXIX

Order Out of Chaos

This chapter is about cleaning up your mental environment. In order to achieve your goals, you will need to remain focused and on task. This won't happen if your thoughts are continuously scattered about without direction. Because every thought you think takes energy to create and maintain, you must begin to systematically remove those thoughts that hold you back.

Orchestrating your environment in a way that brings you positive messages throughout each day is a crucial part of being successful. Our surroundings influence us on many levels. Many things you may not notice or consider can have a significant effect on the way that you typically feel.

Is your house or work space in order and organized, or is it cluttered up with garbage and unfinished tasks? You may be surprised to discover that your personal space is both a cause and effect of your current mental conditioning. A cluttered desk represents a disorganized mind. When you have lots of miscellaneous objects arranged haphazardly, it's very hard to feel good.

Think of your mind as a problem-solving machine. This machine will work through a difficulty until it finds an acceptable resolution.

For example, let's say you have been stuck for some time trying to resolve a certain issue, or you just can't seem to remember something important. After a while, you choose to stop thinking about the issue and move on to something else. Later, when you're in the shower or driving to a regular destination, the answer just pops right into your head.

What happened was that your mind was given a problem, and it became focused on solving it. Even when you turned your attention away from the task, your subconscious was working it out behind the scenes. Some part of your mind continued to work on the issue, even though you had chosen to let it go. Once you began doing a largely subconscious activity, like driving or taking a shower, your inner mind was able to come forward and bring the answer into your conscious awareness.

This is what happens when you have a cluttered environment. Any uncompleted task is like an unsolved problem. Your mind attaches to the task and focuses on resolving it. When you go through life leaving things undone, each one of those activities takes up a piece of mental real estate. Your mind is actually spending energy anticipating the completion of those tasks, even though you're not aware of it. As the days and weeks and months go by, your unfinished business clogs up and bogs down your mind, leaving you less mental energy to focus on achieving your goals.

Start to either do or dismiss unfinished tasks. Design a strategy for doing those things you know need to be done as efficiently as possible. Don't spend any time concerning yourself with tasks that you will never get around to or won't really help you reach your goals. Cross them off of your "to-do" list, so that you can move on to bigger and better things.

When you think about completing a certain task, consider how long it will take you to do so. If it can be completed in just a few minutes, get it done immediately. That way, you'll be finished with the issue and no longer have to think about it. If you know that something will take a bit longer to complete, set up a time to do it in the near future. Most importantly, stick to your plan.

Throw away outdated or useless papers that may be cluttering up your home or work area. Some people have collections of old bills, dead batteries, useless notes and scrap paper from previous months and even years. Their countertops and tables are storage areas for junk. This is just a waste of space and a way of cluttering up your mental landscape. If you have papers lying around that are useful in some way, stack them in a box in the order of priority. Organize the stack so that the most important paper is on top and each one after that decreases in significance. Then, make a point to work the stack down, bit by bit. Perhaps the top paper contains information about a program that can decrease your mortgage payments by 20%. Set a specific time to call the number listed and get the appropriate information, and then get that piece of paper out of your life.

This clearing up principle also goes for material possessions. As time goes on, some people just collect more and more useless stuff. It may be time to get rid of some of your possessions. Make some room in your house by getting rid of items that you no longer use, especially those that are worn out beyond repair.

Sometimes, we just hold on to things that no longer serve us. By refusing to move forward physically, you can actually be holding yourself back mentally as well. Keep in mind the saying, "Out with the old and in with the new."

Here's a good rule to follow. If you haven't worn it, used it or looked at it in more than a year, chances are that you will not do so in the future. Of course, you may come across some useful items that you forgot about. In that case, bring those things back into your normal living or dressing space, and make a point to use them in the near future. Take everything else and sell it, give it away, or throw it away.

Part of this process involves getting organized. When things are in disarray, it's very difficult to feel relaxed and purposeful. Additionally, achieving your goals will involve taking well-planned steps toward your final outcome. If you can't keep your house or your work space in order, how do you expect to manage all of the things that are required to achieve success? See, getting organized actually trains you to develop and maintain useful structures of thought and behavior.

In doing so, you will be improving yourself, not just a room or office. You'll be learning how to manage complex strategies and systems without becoming overwhelmed.

One way to establish order is to create a schedule. Decide what you want to achieve over the next week, month and year. Break these goals down into small manageable tasks that lead to your desired outcome. Some people don't like schedules because they believe them to be restrictive, but a schedule is actually something that frees you. It helps you find more time to be spontaneous and do things you want to do. If you go through your days in a hit-or-miss fashion, you're likely wasting much more time than you realize. You might do a whole bunch of spontaneous activities and, at the end of the day, realize that several important things have been left undone.

This puts you in the cycle of always doing a lot of things, but never getting anything done. There is a big difference between activity and accomplishment. You can spend a lot of energy completing a lot of different tasks and still get nowhere close to achieving your goals. It is easy to get stuck in this pattern because it seems like you're putting in the necessary work.

A schedule will ensure that you're actually doing things that move you forward. You may be surprised to discover how many of your daily activities are really getting you nowhere fast. When you have a schedule, you set aside a specific amount of time for each specific task. Everything you do is tailored toward moving you one step closer to your goal. Start with the end result in mind. Think about where you desire to be in a given amount of time, and then determine what you must do to make what you want a reality. Figure out what you need to acquire or develop to achieve your goals. Keep breaking things down in this way until you have determined the smallest essential steps you can take right now to make progress.

When you clean up your physical space, you're actually removing unnecessary items from your mind. You'll begin to think more clearly and be able to order your ideas. This is necessary for you to achieve the focus needed to get what you want. Remember when we discussed the value of clarity in having a well-defined outcome? It's equally as important to maintain that level of clarity throughout the process. If you want to be more or do better in any area, you must hold yourself to a higher standard. You must develop the discipline to do things in a constructive way. This is why you must align your surroundings with what you want to accomplish.

CHAPTER XXIX:

WORKSHEET

How do unfinished tasks muddle up your mind?

How does cluttered personal space lead to a disorganized mind?

What things have you decided to do that you've never gotten around to completing?

What strategy will you use to start "checking" those things off your list?

How does a schedule actually give you more freedom?

How is it possible to do a lot of things and not get anything done?

How can holding on to unused possessions decelerate your mental growth?

How can you make big goals become more manageable?

How does getting organized train you to manage success?

How does organization relate to focus and clarity?

Treat Others Well

We've already spent time talking about how what you give will all come back to you in return. Now we're going to apply this principle to your interactions with other people. How you treat others will have a massive impact on your ability to receive. Master communicators have known for thousands of years that much of your success is highly dependent on building relationships that support and encourage your efforts. There's almost nothing worthwhile that you can attain without the support of other people. This is why it's ultimately important that you give others the respect, courtesy and consideration that you would want in return.

How you treat others says a great deal about the way you feel about yourself. There's a concept in human psychology known as projection—our tendency to see characteristics in others that we ourselves possess. In fact, many human interactions are based on projection. When you blame, criticize or accuse other people, you often take aim at things about them that, in fact, you do not like about yourself. You may have to take this idea under careful consideration before you recognize it as truth. Look closely, and you'll see that the things you hate most about other people are actually attributes you feel you, in fact, possess. For example, think of someone who always criticizes others for being untidy. On the surface, this person may be the picture of cleanliness. He may be extraordinarily attentive to even minor cases of disorder. But consider what drives this person's behavior. Of course, being organized is important and there's nothing wrong with giving a little advice from time to time. But what causes someone to become obsessed with having other people do things his way? What drives him to demand that others live life on his terms?

People who are genuinely satisfied with their own performance tend not to worry too much about what others are doing, as long as it doesn't hurt anyone else. The person in our example, however, is motivated by something other than genuine concern. On the inside, he believes that being even the smallest bit untidy represents a deterioration of self. He takes having anything out of place as cause to feel shameful and guilty. This person further fears that he may not measure up to this idea of having everything in perfect order. This perceived failure creates an intense internal state of tension and anxiety. The person seeks to relieve this tension by projecting his insecurities onto others. By criticizing other people, he feels as though he is actually taking steps toward resolving that lack of worthiness he feels inside.

Look around you to see what I mean. Have you ever noticed that it is often the most selfish person that talks about how others think only of themselves? The person who acts primarily on impulse condemns others for not thinking things through. Someone with a pushy, aggressive, "Type A" personality will claim that others are nothing but loud-mouthed control freaks. The more that a person feels okay with himself or herself, the less effort he or she will put into judging others. It's okay to notice when things are going wrong. That way you'll know how to set them right. But a critical personality is ego-driven. It comes from that false persona— that mask that we want others to see.

The ego wants to prevent others from seeing those things about ourselves that we believe are flaws. It says, "If I make you out to be bad, then I can feel okay with the way that I am." You have to watch out for doing this, as it's very easy to fall into the trap of trying to "one-up" other people. The ego is a very seductive temptress. Feeling good at the expense of other people can be an alluring proposition, but this feeling is just an illusion. True fulfillment can only come from inside. To find it, you must do what you yourself know is good and right. Criticizing others actually holds you back from producing quality results in your own life. It takes away your energy and causes you to remain focused on someone else's results. The same thing goes for blame. Blame is making people, circumstances or events outside of yourself responsible for whatever predicament you're in.

Of course, people will sometimes do things that can set you back. They will back out of appointments, cancel agreements and leave you hanging out to dry. But to blame is to remove your power from the situation. As long as somebody else remains the problem, you will have to wait for that person to change in order to create better results. This is not the mindset of a winner.

You alone are responsible for the conditions that you stay in. Take a look at that word, "respons-ible." You have the "ability" to "respond" to whatever life brings you. It's not what happens to you, but what you make of it that counts. You can choose how you will respond to whatever comes your way. Of course, others are responsible for their own actions. And, it's true that some of those actions may have sidelined your intentions at one time or another. But blame immobilizes you. It keeps you stuck in a pattern of looking outside yourself for answers. It renders you completely powerless to change anything for the better.

You are fooling yourself if you think that your road to success can only be traveled by trying to change others. That is nothing but a pipe dream. Things won't get better until you get better. Circumstances will not change until you change. It's as simple as that. Blame not only removes your power, but it also puts whomever you are pointing the finger at in the driver's seat of your life. In order to make things happen, you have to put yourself in charge. You can't wait around for anyone else to improve before you start getting positive results. The time to act is now, and you're the one who will make it happen.

Treating others well says many positive things about your character and personality. It's a small mind that puts down other people. You may notice things going wrong in the world and people acting in ways that do not serve them. But your focus must be centered on helping things improve, not talking about what's going wrong with the world.

When you treat people with dignity and respect, you are projecting positive vibes into the universe. Therefore, you will reap the same benefits as you do when you share material wealth. You will be giving your mind the impression that you have more than enough praise, admiration and esteem to go around. By noticing the good in others, you're actually giving yourself permission to enjoy receiving kindness.

Goodwill is mostly displayed in your attitudes and actions, rather than by your words. Haven't you ever had someone give you praise and known he or she didn't really mean it? When you project a false personality, people will pick up on it and learn to resent your phony disguise. However, offering other genuine respect and encouragement raises your level of likeability. If I find that you always find good things to say about other people, I'll know that you'll treat me the same way when I'm not in your presence.

Treating others well also puts you in the right mindset for success. When you can freely appreciate the value that others offer, you are living in a world of abundance. People who do such things are rare and highly regarded. Anyone can put down other people. It doesn't take much creativity to point the finger and blame someone else. It doesn't require any special ability to criticize or condemn someone for doing wrong. But someone who lives in a spirit of gratitude and appreciation demonstrates that he has learned to control both his focus and emotions. Again, how you treat others also determines how you feel about yourself. Remember that we're all a part of the same family. No matter your shape, color or nationality, you and I have more in common than we can ever imagine. We all want to love and be loved, to belong, to contribute and to be a part of something bigger than what we see. These are human qualities, not attributes of gender, race or nationality. Everything that you do to someone else will come back to you. Know that.

One of the ways you can treat others well is by being fair. It's true that "a cheater never wins and a winner never cheats." If you're focused on stepping over people, it will create within you a mindset that is destined to fail, a "scarcity mentality" that makes you think there are not enough resources to go around, so you must get yours before somebody else does. This is a low-level way of thinking that does you more harm than good.

Cheating others is a deceptive practice because it seems to benefit you in the short-term. However, it is in an approach that will fall flat before long. Remember that everything you do is a cause and every cause has its natural effect. Mistreating others earns you a shady reputation and others will treat you in kind. However, a person who's fair and lives according to his or her own values is held in high regard.

People like to associate with others whom they can trust. Many people would rather make a large purchase from the salesperson who is up-front than from one who is just trying to get the sale at any cost.

When pursuing your dreams, you can't play around with trying to take shortcuts. You must provide genuine value to others. You must live with integrity and present yourself as a person of high standards. This is why you should never act toward others in any way that you wouldn't want to experience yourself.

You must want to treat others well because you know that it's the right thing to do. Remember that you will not do really well at things that you're not passionate about. You must know wholeheartedly that being fair produces the greatest good for all. As you begin to positively affect others, doors will open up to you. Certain obstacles will be removed from your path in unexpected ways. You'll run into people who put their hearts, minds and resources at your disposal. The more positive actions you take, the more successful you'll become. But you must be positive in spirit as well as in deed. Otherwise, your words and actions will be sabotaged by internal conflict.

If you were to make a mistake, wouldn't you want others to be compassionate and forgiving? Why not send that out into the world yourself? People are much more likely to be sympathetic to a person who is also forgiving. Have you ever known someone who was extremely critical and judgmental of others? Wouldn't many people look forward to finding fault with that person in return?

Every one of us has an emotional bank account with each person we regularly come into contact with. When you give others reasons to feel good, you make deposits into your account. When you slight people or treat them wrongly, you make a withdrawal. When you give people the best of yourself and you make an effort to add value to the lives of others, you are incrementally putting deposits into your emotional bank account. If you then make a mistake or fall short from time to time, you can be forgiven. You have built up so many deposits that a minor withdrawal can be easily overlooked. But if you generally take advantage of people—if you draw from your reserves on a consistent basis—then even the slightest mistake seems enormous. If you don't put anything in, then you can't afford to take anything out. You may have such a negative balance that even your positive qualities are treated with disregard.

When you do right by others, you don't have to look over your shoulder for the negative backlash that will eventually come. You can sleep well, knowing that no one has any reason to attack you. Of course, you will encounter haters who will try to derail your efforts regardless, but the majority of people you meet will be willing and motivated to help you succeed. We like people who treat us well. Some of the best communicators in history were people who knew how to empower others. Remember that people forget what you tell them, but remember how you make them feel. This will prove evident in every aspect of your life.

Also, consider the fact that we're always telling stories about ourselves. Those stories help define what we believe to be true. When you practice doing good for other people, you're defining yourself as a good person. Therefore, your personal story will be one of a kind, compassionate and warm-hearted individual. You will, naturally, start to feel better and more satisfied with yourself. This is one of the reasons that it's so important to project positivity. You are helping yourself as well as others, and when you act this way toward people, you will inspire them to do the same. This helps make the world a better place, one person at a time. If you can spread a little cheer and good fortune to those around you, it works out better for everyone involved. One character trait that will help you do this is empathy. To be empathetic, you must put yourself in the shoes of another person. This involves making an effort to understand how someone else views the world and what drives other people to do the things that they do. It is the ability to imagine what it's like to actually be another person, to understand what life is like for others and comprehend the challenges they face.

Another way you can treat others well is by developing compassion. Compassion is a desire to relieve the suffering of others. It involves being aware of another's pain, to sense and feel what someone else is going through. Most of us feel compassion for people in our small circle of friends and family. But what I'm talking about here lies in extending that sense of compassion to all people. People really deserve compassion. Everyone needs a little help from time to time. Sure, you probably wouldn't want to do anything for someone you know should and can do it for himself or herself. You are not responsible—and cannot *become* responsible—for other people. But you are responsible for doing things that help humanity evolve, grow and survive. If you have a plan to make it in this world, then you must learn to have compassion for all people.

Sometimes, being good to another person doesn't involve doing anything at all. Listening to someone else may be all it takes to put some good out there into the world. Most of us would much rather talk than listen, which is why this quality can be so difficult to master. Quality listening is a skill that will increase both your understanding and your ability to create wonderful relationships with others. Everyone wants to be listened to. All of us desire to feel significant. We want to be heard, noticed and understood.

So take time to listen to someone else. When you do, make sure that you're really listening, and not simply hearing sounds that come out of another person's mouth. This means that you must put aside your own personal interpretations and simply listen. When another person is talking, many of us are thinking about what we want to say in response. Doing this dramatically cuts down the quality of your listening. Additionally, you'll give out subconscious signals to the other person that you're really not interested in what he or she is saying.

Avoid judging what the other person is talking about or assuming what they will say next. These habits also diminish your ability to listen well. Make an effort to simply open your ears, without judgment, criticism or evaluation. Use your empathy skills to really feel what that the other person is going through. When you talk to others, let them know that you are interested in what they're saying. You can do this with your eyes, facial expressions and body language. But the important thing is that you really become engaged with your companion's ideas. People will instinctively know when you're putting up a fake mask and despise you for doing so. It's much better to practice having genuine concern for those you know and encounter.

Another way to do good for others is by being kind. Many people overlook the value of being nice. But it's one of the best ways to treat people with dignity and respect.

Approach those you meet with a smile on your face. I'm not talking about a fake grimace, when you make a strained effort to slightly lift the corners of your mouth. Give people a real genuine smile, one in which the edges of your eyes crinkle up in delight. You may occasionally smile at a person who returns your expression with a frown. So what? That's that person's problem if he or she wants to work that hard at having a bad attitude. You can only act, think and speak for yourself. You can feel good about your own measures to project a pleasant attitude.

Be helpful. There's nothing wrong with lending a helping hand to someone in need. It's common in our society to believe that a person who wants to achieve a certain outcome should only focus on his or her own needs. But it can be of great value to help someone else manage a difficult situation. Remember that we are a community and no one person is an island. It is important to occasionally extend assistance to other people.

Remember that success involves becoming a person of good character. Think of Ebenezer Scrooge, from Charles Dickens' *A Christmas Carol*. He had an incredible amount of material wealth, but at the same time, he was a miserable, old miser. His days were spent pinching pennies and looking over his shoulder. Is that really the type of life you want? Where is the enjoyment, the passion, the enthusiasm? If you're going to be successful at this game called life, you may as well have a great time while you're playing.

Think about this. Helping others actually protects you from developing many negative characteristics. You cannot become that selfish penny-pinching miser if you are busy trying to help other people. If you were a person of compassion and empathy, you wouldn't be able to exploit others just for a dollar. So by helping others, you help yourself. This is one of the greatest, untapped keys to lifelong happiness and fulfillment. In addition, be compassionate with people. Everyone is on his or her own individual path in life, and different people will move and progress at different speeds. Each person is going through his or her own process and you cannot truly know the purpose of another person's journey.

It can be tempting to criticize those who don't know what you know, who have not taken the time to learn or make substantial progress, but as a wise old saying goes, "When the student is ready, the teacher will appear." A person will only accept new ideas once his or her mind is open and ready to receive them. Until that point, new learning will not take place, no matter how much you push, prod or try to force it.

Jimmy Williams, a legendary athletic trainer known for imparting his students with insights that were elegantly crafted to reflect both sports psychology and important life lessons, would ask an athlete to stretch out one hand with a closed fist. Jimmy would then offer his own car keys and tell the athlete to take them. The catch was that the person to whom Jimmy was talking was not allowed to open his hand. After failing several times to take the keys, the athlete would inevitably admit defeat.

Jimmy would then say, "Just as you cannot receive this object with a closed fist, so you cannot receive any information into a closed mind." You are prepared to make revolutionary changes in your life now, only because you have already opened your mind to greater possibilities.

Some people who are close to you just won't connect with your ambitions, and that's okay. You will have friends who won't be able to make the transition when you do. But you are still responsible for handling your own business. If you spend too much time and energy trying to help others "catch up," you may find yourself being held back from your own true potential.

CHAPTER XXX:

WORKSHEET

How does building relationships help you get what you want?

Explain the meaning of "projection."

What things about others do you find yourself becoming most critical about?

Which of your own unwanted tendencies could this sense of judgment be a reflection of?

Why does the ego persuade you to criticize others?

How does criticizing others inhibit your own ability to succeed?

What special ability do you have to handle whatever life throws at you?

How does blaming others take away your power?

What kinds of things do you tell your mind by treating people well?

Why must your efforts to project goodwill always be genuine?

How does cheating others create a mindset that is destined for failure?

Why is it important to build trust with others?

What is an "emotional bank account?"

Why does it serve you to make as many deposits as possible?

What will you do, from now on, to make your personal story one of kindness and compassion?

CHAPTER XXXI

The "Leap of Faith"

This book has introduced several principles aimed at helping you achieve ever-increasing degrees of success and fulfillment! You may have also noticed that I repeated some ideas and principles one time too many, however, I truly believe that repetition is the building block of learning. All the things you've learned within these pages will only be of benefit to you if you use them. There comes a time when you have to stop contemplating what you're going to do and simply put yourself out there. Nothing different will happen unless you use the tools you've gained by reading the previous chapters and performing the included exercises.

Make reading this book and following the principles contained within it a part of your everyday routine. Yes, it can be very useful to examine the content of these pages more than once. There are a couple of good reasons for this. First of all, when you read a book such as this for the first time, certain concepts will catch your attention. As your mind becomes fascinated with one idea, it may "skim over" what immediately follows. When you go back and read for a second time, the idea that previously caught your attention will be somewhat familiar. Therefore, your conscious mind will have more "space" to examine what comes after it. Have you ever noticed that each time you read a book you notice things about it that you hadn't before? Repetition is one of the keys to gaining functional and comprehensive understanding.

There's another reason why reading this book over and over again is so important. As you go out into the world armed with the techniques and principles contained in these pages, you're going to create some new experiences for yourself. Those experiences will both widen and deepen your capacity to examine and interpret the world around you. Because of this, you will be on a path of continual progression. You will frequently move into higher and more advanced levels of awareness. You will see different things in this book each time you read it because of the attention gap mentioned earlier, but you will also notice new things because you yourself will be a different person.

Have you ever read or listened to something that you didn't understand years ago, only to find that it now makes perfect sense? Most of us have had this type of experience. Here's what happens. When you first review a piece of educational material, you are doing so with the knowledge, understanding and reference points that you possess at that moment. When you come back to the same stuff, you have more of these resources at your disposal. You will be able to see more, because you ARE more.

Take a look into your personal history. You probably saw many things much differently as a child. In many of these cases, the circumstances didn't really change, but you did. So now you have a more mature view of those same situations. The same kind of thing will happen as you continue to read this book.

Taking what I like to call the big "leap of faith" is also crucial for putting these concepts into practice for yourself. You must be utterly convinced that what you want to happen *will* happen when you repeatedly do the right things and when you do the things right. Every successful person has had a moment when he or she has jumped out into the void without seeing where his or her feet will land. You must make up your mind to do exactly the same thing. In reality, there are no guarantees in life. You can't really be 100% certain of what will happen next. Sure, you know that performing certain actions will likely produce particular consequences, but you also know that life can upset even the best-made plans. At some point you must rely on your gut instinct, the part of you that intends to follow through on manifesting the changes you desire. Every person who has achieved greatness trusted or believed at some point in something that was not yet seen.

Harland Sanders, founder of the famous KFC restaurant franchise, didn't set out to pursue his dream until he had reached the age of 65. He was an elderly man who was drawing a Social Security check of only $105 each month. Unsatisfied with his circumstances, Sanders hit the road with little more than a chicken recipe and a dream. He traveled the country, pitching his special formula of herbs and spices to restaurant owners. He slept in his car, wearing the white suit that he's famous for today. People say that he was told "no" 1009 times before anyone ever said yes to his idea. Now KFC franchise operations stretch across the globe and bring in billions of dollars in combined sales each year.

Erik Weihenmayer was born with a rare ocular disease and became completely blind by the age of thirteen. Refusing to use a cane or learn Braille, Erik endeavored to live just as he had before he'd suffered any visual impairment. He took up the sport of wrestling, eventually competing in the National Junior Freestyle Wrestling Championships. Eventually, Erik climbed to the peak of Mount Everest and became the first blind person ever to do so. He had no models to emulate. There were no support systems in place to move him toward these goals. Erik had to create his own path, to leap out into the unknown realm of possibility.

Right now, you have an opportunity to do what has never been done before. You rest on the precipice of greatness and only you can choose what the next move should be. Others may not fully support your ambitions—but that doesn't matter. You may run into sizeable opposition—but so what? You are the commander of your own reality, the orchestrator of this unique and wonderful journey, and it's perfectly okay to get excited about all of this. Heck, I'm excited and I haven't even had the pleasure of meeting you in person yet! This is your life and if you won't allow yourself to get pumped up about that, then what else is there? You are a worthwhile individual. You're smart, talented and probably have much more going for you than you could ever imagine.

Greatness starts right now. It won't happen after you get that new job, after you find a better relationship or get a bigger home. Everything happens right now. There's a saying that goes, "What you will be, you are now becoming." Greatness doesn't just fall into your lap at a certain moment. It is the combined effect of actions taken each minute, each hour and each day. Remember, your current circumstances are a mere reflection of what you've done in the past. And what you will be, have, or be capable of in the future has everything to do with what's going on right now.

So, it's your time to do whatever it is that will make you a whole, that will fill your life with purpose, power and passion. If you had exactly one year to live from now, how would you spend the rest of your time? I'll make a bet that you wouldn't be worrying about all those little inconveniences that concern you now. You probably wouldn't waste any time associating with the people who brought you down or stopped you from doing your best. I'm pretty sure that you would do everything in your power to get the most out of whatever time you had left. Why? Because every single moment would be a precious commodity that you just couldn't bring yourself to throw away.

Well, why don't you go ahead and live that way today? After all, can you really say with 100% certainty that you'll be here next year? None of us are sure how much time we have left. So it's crucial that you make every day count, that you squeeze life for every bit of juice that it can give you. No one else is going to do it for you. In fact, many people would be extremely happy if you were to simply settle for less and go through the motions each day. That way, they wouldn't have to feel so bad about living life in a lackluster fashion.

Remember that small changes make a big difference. You don't have to go out and tackle the world all at once. If all you do is make little improvements, consistently, you will soon be performing at a much higher level than you are now.

That said, however, it's better to err on the side of boldness. There will be many times when you won't know how far you can go until you go too far. This is not to say that you should be reckless or disregard good sense, but you have to be willing to take life on, to go at it with everything you've got, and you have way more to give than you think.

You have an enormous reserve of potential just waiting to be released. People often do much, much less than what they are capable of. Most often, we stop because *we* think we should—not because some outside force prevents progression.

What I want you to do now is simply dream about your desired outcome. Let your imagination run wild. See yourself as you want to be, with all of the resources, abilities and characteristics that you most want to have. Your vision is your roadmap, the compass that you will use to navigate everyday life. Consider what you would do, at this moment, if you knew that you could successfully overcome anything that comes your way. What is your inner sense of direction encouraging you to explore? Everything that you are seeking is already within you.

Think about a person who you admire for any reason. When you really get down to it, you respect things in other people that you yourself already possess within. Say you want to be an excellent communicator and have a high opinion of someone who seems to move the emotions of certain crowds. At the same time, you might not have much interest in another person's ability to connect with those to whom you do not relate. In these types of situations, you are employing the same concept of projection that we discussed earlier. Only, now, you are seeing your own positive qualities in others.

Certain characteristics do not inspire you because those qualities are not a part of your personal makeup. You pay special attention to the positive attributes of others because those things resonate with you on a deep level. Those same qualities that you admire are inside of you right now. You are simply waiting to encounter that which you deem worthy to trigger your inner greatness. Now is the time to get started on what you want. No matter where you are in your life right now, you can get to where it is that you want to go. Your time is now. Don't get caught up with waiting around until everything is ideal. The perfect moment will never come. Just get things going—then allow momentum to help you pick up speed.

See, you are always creating results. Even attempting to do nothing is still a choice, a decision that is likely to affect your life in ways you don't want. Every choice creates consequences. You simply can't avoid that reality. In life, you're always on the playing field. You can either watch from the sidelines or go out and get into the game. Don't get caught up in the "I need more confidence trap." This is a disordered form of logic that says, "I'll do what I want once I've built up my confidence."

The big problem with this way of thinking is that confidence can be linked to certainty. The more certain that you are about your ability to perform a task well, the more confident you feel about doing so. And you only become certain about your ability to do something by doing it over and over again. Most people want to put the cart before the horse. They think that they'll start taking action once they have the confidence to follow through, but you will only get the "confidence" by repeatedly doing what it is that you are unskilled at right now. That's where learning to play with life comes into effect. Start approaching each day as an adventure, an experiment in which you get to step back and curiously observe how you can impact the world around you. You must develop the ability to draw enthusiasm from within yourself. The outside world won't always support your goals, but you already have inside you everything you need to lead a life of passion, purpose and fulfillment.

You are the kind of person who deserves the success you want to enjoy. How do you know that? Well, it's because you have an unyielding desire, an enormous passion to create what you desire. That passion comes from inside, from a place where your very purpose for living exists. You are the only one who has the capacity to make those dreams a reality.

American automotive pioneer Henry Ford once said, "If you think you can do a thing, or think you can't do a thing, you're right." This means you will produce results that are congruent with whatever you believe to be true about yourself. That's why it's so important to set goals that align with your values, with who you are beneath superficial and material objectives.

When you know, on a deep level, who you are and where you're going, life takes on a brand new sense of meaning. The clearer you make the image of your future goals, the more direct your path to success will become. Your brain is an instruction-absorbing mechanism. The more real and distinct you make your vision of success, the more your vitality for life will increase. Get really clear about your image of success. Think about having the life that you desire. Imagine how you will feel when you have what you want. Consider everything, including what you will see, hear, feel, smell and taste. This will give your brain an exact set of instructions about what you intend to find in the outside world.

Don't be afraid to make your dreams bigger and better than they've ever been before. Famed motivational speaker Les Brown once said, "Shoot for the moon. Even if you miss, you'll land among the stars." Most people settle for much too little in life. Remember that you are one of a kind and you have a reason for being here. You were created to bring into existence that which is in your heart.

Each moment, you are writing a new line of your personal story. Keep in mind is that you are the author. You have the power to change the script at any time. You are the director, producer, writer and main character. If you don't like the way things are turning out, you can change roles and adjust the story line mid-stream. Isn't it time that you start playing the hero instead of the victim? Wouldn't you prefer living out a magnificent adventure instead of a tale of boredom and disappointment? Becoming the person that you want to be is as simple as making a decision. The process of doing that may be difficult at times, but once you make a firm commitment to be, do, or have more, you're already on your way. When you do the things that lead to success, periods of discomfort should be celebrated. They represent the opening stages of your personal evolution, a process that is transforming you into someone who is capable of much more.

You have everything going for you. If you don't succeed at achieving your goals, you'll probably be no worse off than you are now. In fact, you will have gained all the lessons that come with living a life of purpose. If you continue with your quest, if you can meet with setbacks and not be discouraged, the odds are in your favor. You have the ability to produce results. The one question really is: Are you willing to do what it takes to get what you want? Chances are that there are people who now enjoy the type of life that you want. Many of them started out with fewer resources than you have at your disposal. If they could do it, then why can't you?

All successful people have mental stamina—the resolve to go through whatever it takes to reach a desired outcome. This ability is inside of you. All of us have had the experience of wanting something so badly that we just wouldn't take no for an answer. Think of how children behave when they are focused on getting a new toy, having a special treat or going to a fun place. They are relentless and will go after what they want from every angle. Take this attitude when it comes to what you want out of life. Success is not for the faint of heart. It's for those who are willing to go after it and not give up until victory is achieved. And remember to keep contribution in mind. Certain parts of your road to success will be paved by other people. Sow goodwill and you will reap support that will come to you in ways you could never imagine.

Stay hungry. Reaching your goal is just one stop on the road to success. Part of enjoying a higher quality of life is learning how to keep whatever you earn and produce even greater things for yourself. Living a mediocre existence may be somewhat uncomfortable. But it feels even worse to come from such a position, get a small taste of achievement, and then return to a life of discontent. Remember that the world is always changing and evolving. The things that got you to a certain position of achievement may not be enough to keep you there after a while. This is why it's important to remember that success is a continual process. You must be just as committed to your ongoing growth and personal development as you are to accomplishing what you desire.

Take advantage of opportunities because they will open up doors to you that help you move forward. Doing well at small things, every day, will help you accomplish big goals. Singing at a local charity event may lead you to meet someone who can put you on a bigger stage. Showing your crafts at the monthly bazaar can put your work in the face of large-scale retailers. Do some custom landscaping for a friend and the entire neighborhood may come-a-calling. Remember, people know other people, and those people know people, and so on. Do what you do best, and do it as well as you can, every single time.

We already know that taking consistent action is essential to the process of creating the life you want. But action, alone, isn't enough. You have to "show up" when it's time to do your thing. This means you have to make it a point to bring your best self to the table, every time. You must be prepared to take advantage of good fortune when it pops-up. As twentieth century social reformist William M. Young, Jr. once said, "It's better to be prepared for an opportunity and not have one than to have an opportunity and not be prepared."

The sad thing is that most people quit going after something just before attaining what they want. If you just push a little harder, if you just go a little further, success is just around the corner. It's said that the darkest hour of night comes just before daybreak. This is also true when it comes to our lives. Often, we face our hardest times just before opportunity opens up. It's as though life is presenting you with a final challenge just to make sure that you really "want it."

When things seem their worst, you're likely on the verge of getting something great. So don't stop! Former British Prime Minister Winston Churchill once said, "If you're going through hell, keep going." Don't stop when things are their toughest. You don't want to stay there. You've gone much too far to give up now. If you've already gone through some really hard times, then you might as well get a benefit from it. Don't go through all that suffering for nothing. You deserve to get something out of the pain you endure. That's one of the reasons why it's so important to persist.

This is true even if you don't consider yourself to be the best. You may not be the fastest, the smartest, the most charismatic or the most educated. But if you keep going when others give up, you'll find yourself ahead of the pack before long. See, drive and motivation will take you places that talent cannot.

It's easy to do things when things are easy. They key lies in doing what you know is right at times when it's not comfortable. Everyone who wants what you want can do what feels good. But those who achieve mastery will have developed the ability to perform at their best despite personal challenges. When an athlete wants to become stronger, she must become comfortable with being uncomfortable. She must make the decision to press on when her body says, "Stop." She must make it a point to push herself to new, unrealized, degrees of performance.

Remember that you have a big "WHY"—a reason for going through whatever comes your way. So don't go after a goal just for the purpose of achieving it. Do it to be an example to your kids, better the community, break a generational pattern of poverty or whatever your "WHY" happens to be. Instead of trying to push yourself forward with logic, place your purpose in front of you and be led. Logic and reason often fall to the wayside when one is put under tremendous pressure, but passion and purpose will cause you to look into the face of seemingly impossible odds and say, "I'm going to do it anyhow!"

Life is not a trial run. As far as we know, you only get one go-around. Because no one knows when the end will come, you have absolutely no time to waste. In truth, it doesn't make any sense to prolong going after whatever it is that you want. What would you be waiting for—next month, next year, next decade? In the end, that would only give you less time to enjoy the fruits of your labor.

The funny thing is that the older you get, the faster the years seem to go by. Before you know it, you could be looking back and wondering, "Where did the time go?" Too many of us simply take time and life for granted. We just assume that opportunity will wait around until we feel comfortable enough to grab it. But certain windows of possibility are closing even as you read this book. True, it's never too late to start pursuing your dreams, but procrastination can make things much harder on you than they need to be.

Take, for example, the person who knows he should lose weight, but spends a decade waiting to do anything about it. He may only decide to take action after having a heart attack or becoming diabetic.

This person can still lose the weight, but the road to his success will now be harder to travel. He may get to his ideal body size, but continue to suffer from the physical damage caused by being overweight for so long. Had he started getting in shape years earlier, however, this could all have been avoided.

If you know that you should eat better, start doing so now. If you want to save money, begin putting away a little something out of each check. You don't have to do anything drastic. Do something that you know you can do just to get the ball rolling.

We all have the same amount of time to live each day. Successful people simply use their time more intentionally than those who are not. Don't just go through life doing time. Instead, make time work for you. Think about how much time most of us spend in a car or riding some sort of public transportation. What about when you're doing household chores that don't really require any concentration? If you use those times to spend a total of just one hour, each day, listening to some educational material, you will have acquired over 365 hours of additional learning each year.

Do you need some extra training in order to achieve what you want? With today's technology, you can go to school in your spare time, without taking away from any of your daily responsibilities. How great is that? You have what you need, right now, to start moving in the right direction. All you need to do is rely on your natural creative faculties to overcome any obstacles you face.

I once saw Musician/Vocalist/Producer Wyclef Jean speaking to a classroom of so-called "underprivileged" kids on television. He said that there was absolutely no excuse for not achieving your dreams. Wyclef talked about growing up in Haiti, living in a small shack with dirt floors and barely having enough to survive. At times, he and his siblings were reduced to eating red clay from the floor of his "home" for food. He said that if someone with his background could make it, then anyone there could as well.

Here was a man who started out with less than most of us would consider to be nothing. He was extremely poor and came into a strange country where he didn't even speak the language. But he loved music and wanted to know everything he could about songwriting and production. Years later, he was a multi-platinum recording artist. When asked how he got the money to study English and take lessons in music, Wyclef replied, "The library is free."

You have resources at your disposal. All you have to do is think outside of the box and take the "leap of faith." Think about what Wyclef said about the library. Almost every town has one and they're free to use. You can go in and learn almost whatever you want—for nothing! How many people look right past such opportunities and create imaginary obstacles for themselves?

Where you start does not decide where you will end up. Each person only gets twenty-four hours in a day. All that really matters is how you choose to use yours. When you get committed to using your twenty-four hours in a purposeful way, you'll begin to see positive things happening quickly.

See, without doing this, you'd likely be managing your days in a nonchalant fashion. You'd just watch whatever appears on TV, listen to whatever comes on the radio and spend free time doing aimless activities.

What would happen if you made choices about what to allow into your mind, based upon your values, goals and purpose? How quickly would your life change if you merely learned to control your focus in this way? Well, you'd immediately find yourself getting more done and doing more useful things that help you feel good.

Think about and speak of yourself in empowering terms. How you view yourself will set the mentality that you take into life. Instead of thinking, "I've still got fat to lose," try "I am achieving my ideal weight and body image." Be "a singer," not just someone who's "trying to make it in music." You're not just "hoping for a promotion," you're "training for a management position." Get the idea firmly in mind that you're already on your way. That is one of the first steps to making good things happen for yourself. And make sure that you hustle at whatever you do to achieve your goals.

Robert Schuller once said, "Tough times never last, but tough people do." Of course, it's easier to stay in bed and sleep than it is to get up at 5 a.m. to work on your goal. It's easier to grab a bucket of fast food after work than it is to go to the gym and grab a bar full of weights. It's easier to say, "I tried it and things didn't work out" than "I'm going to get this done no matter what." And make sure you expect to produce good results. You deserve it. The average person might say, "I'll believe it when I see it." But I want you to take exactly the opposite outlook. As you seek to create your ideal life, know that "You'll see it, when you believe it." Remember that you get back whatever you put out into the universe. Therefore, you must project the good that you want to see.

CHAPTER XXXI:

WORKSHEET

Why is now the time that you must walk into your greatness?

What are the first steps that you will take to move beyond the circumstances in which you live now and toward those that live in you?

What are the thought, habits and relationships you need to cultivate in order to achieve your goals?

What things are you willing to do now that you've never done before?

What action steps can you create from some of the key concepts you've learned in this book?

What resources do you have at your disposal that you may not have considered until now?

How will your life have changed by this time next year?

In five years?

Ten?

What are some reasons for pursuing your dream that are stronger than any fears you may have now?

CHAPTER XXXII

Personal Commitment

One of the most important things you can do is develop the quality of self-discipline. Discipline is the ability to make yourself do what you need to, despite how you feel at the moment. All successful people have learned to do this. You cannot achieve anything worthwhile and lasting without mastering control of your own conduct.

In fact, when it comes to personal qualities that help you succeed, self-discipline may stand above all others. You could learn every technique, strategy and principle in the world. However, if you can't follow through and take whatever actions are necessary, none of information you get will do you any good.

Discipline is the opposite of impulsiveness. An impulsive person simply takes any action that comes to his or her mind. His or her behavior is not value-driven. This type of person does not take time to determine whether what he or she does today will serve his or her ambitions in the long run.

Compulsive people often fool themselves into believing that what they do is on track with what they want. They mistake action for progress and, therefore, steadily lead themselves down a path that goes nowhere.

The highly disciplined individual, however, does not lead a life based solely on immediate gratification. She enjoys her work, but insists on taking actions that lead her to higher levels of achievement. Self-disciplined people make good decisions now that will lead to even greater results in the future. They know that what will happen is simply cumulative effect of certain actions taken, in the moment, each day. Does that make any sense?

Let me give you an example. Suppose you want a better job, but don't yet possess the skill-set needed to perform in another position. You need to undergo some training, which costs money you simply don't have at the moment. Furthermore, it will take time for you to go to school and learn the things that you need to move ahead. Let's say that you also lead a very busy social life. You eat out for dinner five days a week and party with co-workers on Saturday night. You enjoy this lifestyle and don't want to give it up. Yet you also know that you'll never be satisfied at your current level of employment. What do you do?

Let's look at two possible scenarios. In the first, you are playing the role of a largely impulsive individual. You sign up for vocational classes, but are determined to continue leading the life that you know. Soon, you find out that both working and partying don't leave you much time to study. You are tired all of the time and can't really concentrate when hitting the books. On top of that, your nighttime spending habits have left you in financial hardship. Before long, you can no longer pay for classes and have to drop out of school.

In the second example, you have developed the invaluable quality of self-discipline. You still enjoy going out, but only once or twice a week. You get to bed earlier and make sure you have plenty of time and energy to go over the material covered each week in class. Even though you've cut down on social activities, you know that the end reward far outweighs any momentary inconvenience.

Can you see why discipline is not only a very important quality to have, but is absolutely essential to getting what you want out of life?

And the more you practice being in control of your everyday actions, the more this ability will continue to grow over time.

Self-discipline is, in fact, mastery over one's own emotions and behaviors. And self-discipline actually engenders self-appreciation. We've all had moments of doing something that creates only a short-term benefit. Rarely do we feel very good about ourselves afterward, unless the gain we receive is something trivial or particular to the occasion.

Inside, each of us knows that we must do certain things that are somewhat uncomfortable in order to succeed. When we fail to perform these tasks, a little bit of our self-respect is diminished on some level. Do the thing that deserves doing, however, and you will find yourself feeling a little more dignified and committed.

Discipline is a habit, just like thousands of other things you do each day. It may seem difficult to break out of your normal routines at first. But when you do it again and again, the new pattern of behavior will eventually become natural. In fact, it will be just as easy to do those things that work in your favor as it used to be to follow your old course of action.

Say you want reduce the amount of sugary drinks you consume on a regular basis. You could do this by replacing soft drinks and other sweet beverages with water. At first, you may feel as though you are deprived of the sharp flavors you have become accustomed to. After a few weeks, however, you'll likely find water to be quite refreshing and soothing to the palate. In fact, the thought of having a sugar-filled drink might turn you off.

This is why it's so important that you push through those initial stages of unease when pressed to do something positive that falls outside of your comfort zone. You won't know what you can do or accomplish until you dare to venture beyond what you know. Doing this takes a substantial amount of self-discipline.

In actuality, discipline is what leads to the accomplishment of anything worthwhile. That may involve approaching a difficulty "head-on" instead of making excuses or rationalizing away your results. It could be creating a schedule and sticking to it, as opposed to letting daily distractions take you off course. But discipline is a quality that can only be developed through practice.

Disciplined people don't necessarily have to *like* doing all of their tasks. They simply recognize the value of completing tasks that lead to progress. They then take whatever actions need doing, despite outside opposition and internal emotional resistance. You must be able to do the same thing if you want to move out of where you are and into where you want to be. Sometimes, you must stand up to yourself, for yourself, within yourself. We all occasionally hear that little voice inside, saying things like "Give up now before it's too late" and "Turn around. Head back to safety. You're just not made for this." But at times like these you must take control of that inner conversation. You must learn to lead your mind and not let it lead you. That voice really isn't yours anyway. It is that of your father, mother, teacher and peer group. It is the expression of things implied to you by your culture, government, society and mainstream media. It's very appropriate, at times, to disregard that critical part of your mind or simply force it to stay quiet. In fact, you may have to tell yourself "Shut Up!" from time to time. Remember that thoughts are simply thoughts. They don't identify you or necessarily reveal any truth about what you're capable of.

Your happiness is not determined by what happens to you, but by the interpretations and meanings you give to whatever occurs. Those negative ideas that creep into your mind will take over if you let them. Because our habitual mental patterns run so quickly and automatically, most of us never take time to consider what effect those thoughts are producing.

Your inner world is, in fact, your home. It's where you live twenty-four hours a day. Your beliefs and habitual thoughts determine what you see and how you evaluate the world around you. This is why it's important for you to think purposefully, to intentionally decide what you will and will not let into your mind.

People often doubt their positive thoughts and give far too much credit to the negative ones. They don't realize that it's just as easy to essentially doubt the doubt—to deny disempowering messages that emerge without warning. You could simply backtrack and erase those thoughts. When you find yourself indulging in self-criticism, say something like, "Okay STOP! Rewind. Delete that." Or you could eliminate the tendency to find fault with yourself by asking questions. Often, negative thoughts come in absolutes, such as: "I can't ever get anything right" or "Things just never work out for me." Really? Never? With a little thought, you can see that determinations like these are just plain silly at best.

You get lots of things right every day. You are skilled in areas that others are not. So when these kinds of thoughts come up, ask yourself a few pointed questions. You might go with something like "What things have I learned to do in my life that seemed very difficult to master at first?" Or, you could ask "What unexpected moments of good fortune have come to me through life?" If you take time to think, you will probably uncover numerous examples that counter the negative self-talk. On top of this, you will build up your ability to deflect self-criticism and evaluate things more rationally.

It's time to "jump-start" your life. Everything has to keep moving forward. That's the only way to get whatever you can out of life. This is your moment. It's all about what happens right now. I want you to be in a place where you're squeezing the last drop of "juice" out of every single day. But you have to make things happen for yourself. When life attempts to throw you off course, it is your job to find new avenues, new opportunities. After all, anything can and will happen—duties will increase, laws will change, and people will change. But it's what you do with these kinds of circumstances that really make the difference. Part of your curriculum, therefore, is to develop the mindset of a champion. The time to realize your dreams has finally come, but you have to get your mind in the right place first. Who you are is far beyond what you ever imagined.

In order to discover that, however, you must give it everything you've got. In order to reach a level of peak performance, a transformation must take place, and it all starts inside of your mind.

Your mindset can either build you up or break you down. One of the keys to finding motivation is to use what you already have. Most of us feel inspired several times a day to do something positive for our lives, but only a select few actually act on that sense of inspiration. You have to switch your mental attitude from that of one who merely dreams big to that of a person who takes action, specifically, hard action. As the old saying goes, "Hard work will always beat talent, when talent doesn't work hard." Everyone loves an underdog story because each one demonstrates how unstoppable the determined human spirit really is.

You must completely believe in what you do and put that belief into motion on a continuous basis. You can't rely on luck to make your dreams a reality. Preparation is the true key to success in this context. It doesn't matter how hard you have to push—how far you have to stretch—because in the end, it's all worth it. Without risk, there is no reward, plain and simple. In order to do anything great—whether that is becoming a great husband, entrepreneur, athlete or motivator—you must be willing to put yourself on the line. Being successful takes guts; make no mistake of that, but you already possess whatever resources you need to turn your innermost dreams into reality.

There may be times when you seem to fall flat on your face, but if you never put yourself out there, you will have exactly a 0% chance of achieving success. There's a saying that goes, "You will never know how far you can go until you go too far." What would happen if you gave it your all—if you left absolutely everything you have on the table?

This process is about maximizing your potential. It's not about giving 50, 60 or 75 percent. The great ones don't leave anything in reserve. They view every moment as an opportunity to become stronger, better and more effective. If somebody is going to excel—be in fantastic health, have a wonderful family life; make lots of money—why "shouldn't" it be you? You could come up with excuses, but excuses will never give you positive results. They are just a way of keeping you from your true potential.

What you feel that you lack in physical strength, intellectual ability or training can always be supplemented with enough effort. But if you sell yourself short, you can never fulfill your true life's purpose. And when you think about what's been holding you back until now, you will realize that it was merely your own mistaken perception about who you are. Everything in your life, in fact, is about who you think you are. The only thing that has any real power over you is your own self-concept. No matter where you are in life right now, someone else has started from there and gone on to do really amazing things. The hard part is deciding to take responsibility and become the captain of your own ship, instead of remaining "just another passenger."

On the next page is a contract that I'd like you to read and sign, expressing your personal commitment to achieve your goals and to start taking action right now. This is a binding contract. By signing this, you are agreeing to eliminate any excuses and take on the mindset that you will produce the results that you want—no matter what happens.

Personal Success Contract

I, _____, hereby agree to go beyond the story of my past, to take risks that are designed to move me toward a higher quality of life. I promise to interpret any perceived failure as an instrument of learning, something that moves me forward in pursuit of my dreams. I will associate with people who have made it to the other side of challenges I face right now. I will upgrade my goals to the point where reaching them will make me stretch well beyond my comfort zone. I am willing to do things I've never done before in order to have what I've never had. I will be persistent, perseverant and hold myself fully responsible for making my dreams a reality. I now know that the future lies in my hands alone. Nobody will care about my success more than me. No one will be more passionate about my vision than I am. I will think about what I want as though I already have it, like I am already the person I am committed to becoming. While it may be difficult for me to believe that I can have, do or be anything that I want to right now, I understand that this is all part of my previous mental conditioning. My current limits only represent the boundaries of my inherent levels of my understanding at this moment. I am committed to learning whatever I need to accomplish whatever gives me a true sense of purpose. I will not settle anymore because I have the infinite ability to create success and abundance. The past is gone. The future hasn't arrived. All I've got is now. Now is the time to step up and take back control. I choose to step up. I choose to fight, and keep fighting to win. Today I am taking a decision, and I will honor it because I know that what I want is worth it. Because I know that I am worth it.

I affirm all of these things, here and now.

Name   Signature   Date